HOW TO GET YOUR TEENAGER OUT OF THEIR BEDROOM

ANITA CLEARE

HOW TO GET YOUR TEENAGER OUT OF THEIR BEDROOM

The ultimate tools and strategies for understanding, connecting with and being there for your teenager

WATKINS

Sharing Wisdom
Since 1893

How to Get Your Teenager Out of Their Bedroom
Anita Cleare

First published in the UK and USA 2024 by
Watkins, an imprint of Watkins Media Limited
Unit 11, Shepperton House
89–93 Shepperton Road
London N1 3DF

enquiries@watkinspublishing.com
Design and typography copyright © Watkins Media Limited 2024
Text copyright © Anita Cleare 2024

Commissioning editor:Ella Chappell
Editorial manager: Daniel Culver
Designer: Karen Smith

A CIP record for this book is available from the British Library

ISBN: 9781786788665 (Paperback)
ISBN: 9781786788887(Ebook)

1 3 5 7 9 10 8 6 4 2

Set in Candara
Printed and bound by CPI Group (UK) Ltd, Croydon, CR0 4YY

www.watkinspublishing.com

. . . a little help, a little hope and someone who believes in you.

CONTENTS

INTRODUCTION

All teens are different. Some skip lightly through the teenage years making good decisions, staying close to their parents and remaining open to positive influences. Others take a rockier route via risk-taking and defiance of authority. And some just shut up shop and retreat to their bedrooms. It's hard to be sure which children will take which route. Over the ten or more years of adolescence, your teenager might do a bit of all three.

However, if you've picked up this book, it's likely that your teen is in withdrawal mode. Maybe they have withdrawn from the wider world, or just from you. Maybe they have separated physically, setting up a teen-only domain in their bedrooms. Or perhaps they have retreated into eyerolls or rudeness or monosyllabic answers (interlaced with random cuddles or lashes of anger). Some teens refuse to participate in family life at all and carve out a parallel existence within the home. Others are prepared to tag along on your family outings but withdraw into their phones. Others are so resentful at being dragged along that they sabotage everyone else's enjoyment and make you wish they'd stayed in their rooms.

In most cases, this teen withdrawal is simply a chrysalis moment, a temporary phase from which teenagers eventually emerge as lovely young adults. But it is also the time when teens are at their most vulnerable. Suddenly their bodies are changing, sex is on their minds, schoolwork becomes more demanding, friendships are more complex and they are faced with a series of seemingly life-changing decisions about their future. It is a time of high stakes and sustained stress. Most teens grapple with self-doubt and insecurities – especially around their appearance and fitting in – and many teens experience a dip in their self-esteem. For some, struggles with mental health completely take over.

The problem is, if your teen won't talk to you, it's hard to know what's going on or how to help. At this time when teens are at their most vulnerable, they can also be hardest to reach.

Whether a teenager's withdrawal is just a passing phase or the result of underlying struggles, we can't just leave them to it. The relationship between parents and teenagers really matters. We know that the presence of a caring, supportive adult is a vital factor in helping teens grow into happy and successful young adults. The aim of this book is to help you be that adult. To help you find ways to understand what's going on and maintain a connection – so you can be the parent your teenager needs (even if, right now, they don't want anything to do with you).

In the chapters that follow, you will find concrete tips on how to bridge the divide of teenage withdrawal, build a good relationship with your teen and nurture their wellbeing despite that often-closed bedroom door. The focus will be on real-world wins and small everyday actions – things you can take away and do today that will make a difference. I'll give you a blueprint for how to get a reluctant teen to spend time with you (and explain why it really matters that you persevere in this) and lay out guidelines on how to communicate effectively (without nagging!). There will be strategies for tackling some of the tricky issues that often accompany teen withdrawal, like compulsive gaming, obsessive phone use and social anxiety. I will draw on neuroscience and developmental psychology to help you understand what's going on inside your teenager's brain. And I'll bring the lessons from my 20 years of experience in supporting families to help you find parenting strategies that really work, whether your child is at the beginning of their journey through adolescence (at 11 years old) or right in the thick of the teenage years.

The key messages and strategies in this book will help you support your teenager no matter what challenges they face. However, there are many issues I haven't delved into and for which you will need specialist support (such as gender dysphoria and eating disorders, to name just two). I go into detail about anxiety (chapter 7) and depression (chapter 8) as these are so prevalent among modern teens – especially among teens who withdraw – and anxiety and depression often coincide with other teen struggles.

This book is not for teenagers to read. It's aimed at parents (both mums AND dads) or anyone occupying the role of primary caregiver to a teenager. Other family members and professionals working with teenagers will find this book useful but, truthfully, I'm not writing it for them. In my experience, the relationship teenagers have with their teachers, coaches or other family members is often different from the way they behave with parents. It's parents they need to separate from in order to become independent young adults – which is why your teen might gladly accept wise advice from a coach but throw exactly the same advice back at you with an added helping of hurtfulness.

There will be lots of honesty. None of us get through the teenage years without committing some real howlers (it's not just our teens who have to cope with changes and difficult emotions). I'll be sharing tips I have picked up from other parents and telling you a little of my own story along the way – not because I did everything right (far from it) but because I want you to know that it's OK to make mistakes and that there are ways back from even the toughest of ruptures.

This book has emerged from some of my most powerful personal and professional experiences. The idea first came to me with an article I wrote describing my personal sense of loss and rejection as my teenage son withdrew:

> Some days, I miss my teenage son so much it makes me cry. He hasn't gone anywhere. He still lives in my house. I still see him every day. But he doesn't want to be with me anymore. He doesn't really want to speak to me at all.*

The response to this article was overwhelming. It generated hundreds of comments from parents saying how much they identified with it. Many emailed me directly to tell me their stories and offer me hope and advice. I knew I had hit a nerve, but at the time I was nowhere near ready to find the emotional distance to write this book. It was all too raw.

Then, my son was diagnosed with depression and anxiety and things got a lot worse. Apart from going to school and occasional hair-raising risk-taking with his friends, he barely came out of his room. Our personal journey through teenage mental ill-health was long and hard, taking in panic attacks, suicidal ideation, self-harm and deceit. I got so much wrong. But I also learnt so much along the way about how to create a positive connection out of teenage disconnect.

Most parents don't have to face these extremes. Your teenager might just be absorbed in gaming, a little obsessive about their digital social lives or feeling self-conscious. Or perhaps they are simply asserting their independence through that closed bedroom door. Hopefully, you will find reflected in these pages behaviours and challenges you recognize and the tools you need for understanding, connecting with and being there for your teenager, whatever is going on for them.

What you won't find in this book is blame. Wherever you are right now, blame is not going to help. What's needed is understanding. I want you to finish this book with a greater understanding of what's going on inside you and your teenager, and have a clear mission for parenting your way through it (with practical ideas for putting that into practice).

---

* You can find this article on the *Huffington Post* UK website.

Most of all, I want you to finish this book with hope. Because it won't always be like this. No matter how hard things feel right now, no matter how distant, disengaged, rude or sad your teenager is today, their future is bright, and they will blossom into lovely young adults. It's vital that you believe that. Make it your mantra. Record it onto your phone and play it to yourself every day. By believing in their bright future, you are believing in them. And no matter what your teenager says or does, they need to feel that you believe in them. They may not be grateful for your efforts (or understand the true cost of them), but your support makes all the difference.

With that in mind, here's a little hope to get us started.

PERSONAL STORY
A TALE OF TWO MOTHER'S DAYS

MOTHER'S DAY (TEEN AGE 15)

I wake up in the morning, the teens are still asleep. I know my husband will have reminded them it's Mother's Day today. I'm certain he will have helped them out with money for presents and done a bit of nagging (he wouldn't want me to miss out).

One of the teens is up early and off to a sports match. After some conspiratorial shuffling in another room, he kisses my cheek and hands me some tulips and a homemade card that reads "Thanks for being the best mum." Then he's off. The tulips are from the corner shop – but he went and bought them himself, my husband tells me.

The other teen doesn't emerge from his room until lunchtime. There is more shuffling and some sharp voices. He disappears back to his room without saying hello.

I head out to the kitchen where I find a jug with three different sized daffodils picked from outside our back door, plus a packet of my favourite dark chocolate buttons. I'm pretty sure this was my husband's backup present in case one of the teens forgot.

There's also an envelope with the word "Mum" on it, which I open. It contains the delivery note for the chocolate buttons straight from the parcel. He didn't even look at it, just wrote my name on it.

I spend the rest of the day feeling abject, and binge eat the chocolate buttons fighting back the tears.

MOTHER'S DAY (TEEN AGE 18)

I am away for the weekend in the mountains with one of the teens and the family dog. He still tends to opt out of family activities, but we have developed a tradition of going away together for a weekend every few months, just the two of us. I had forgotten it would be Mother's Day when I booked this trip (to be honest, I've rather disinvested from the whole charade).

He comes down, makes himself breakfast, and we chat about plans for the day. He seems to have forgotten it is Mother's Day, so I let it lie. We are enjoying ourselves and this is precious.

We are about to head off for a walk when he hands me a card. "Happy Mother's Day", he says and gives me a hug. I open the card and read it.

"Dear Mum, Thank you for always being there for me and always trying your hardest. You are the best mum I could ask for. I'm so lucky to have such a caring and loving mum and to be as close as we are. Thank you for putting up with me all this time and always having faith in me, my life would be very different without you. I love you very much."

I burst into tears.

CHAPTER 1

WHAT HAS HAPPENED TO MY CHILD?

Does it feel like your child isn't quite "themselves" these days? That they've put on an ill-fitting costume belonging to some other teenager? Are they behaving in ways that go completely against everything you have tried to instil in them? When the teenage years arrive, the change can be abrupt and disorienting. It might feel like the child you knew and loved has morphed into a completely different person (and not necessarily one you like).

We were always so close.

This isn't like them at all.

He's so rude to me these days.

She won't even talk to me.

The teenage years are all about transition, and change is seldom comfortable. What you see in front of you isn't your child acting out or going off track. This is your child doing their absolute best to grapple with the profoundly unsettling biological, psychological and environmental changes that arrive with the onset of adolescence.

Teens have major developmental "work" to do. The adolescent decade* is when children must work out who they are and learn to take their place as young adults in society. And they are driven through this transition by forces beyond their control. Just like a toddler compelled to pull themselves to standing to bounce on their legs and prepare themselves for walking, teenagers are impelled to flex the muscles that will lead them into independent young adulthood.

Most of us go into shock when we are first faced with an alien teen in our child's place. But denying or dismissing this change isn't going to help. We need to get to know this new young adult who is emerging and support them to grow. And, to do that, curiosity is essential. We need to wonder, genuinely, about what might be going on inside this new evolving person because what might seem like bad attitude or selfishness from the outside, looks different when we peek inside and understand where it's coming from.

So, let's take a look at what's going on inside your teenager.

The teenage developmental project

We'll begin with the big picture. If the teenage years are the bridge between childhood and adulthood, what are the major changes that teens need to accomplish?

- **Children** live in homes provided for them by adults who care for them and take responsibility for all aspects of their health, wellbeing and education.
- **Adults** are expected to find their own homes with people of their own choosing and are responsible for providing for their own needs.

---

* This is from the age of 11 to 22, or thereabouts.

In order to transition from a child to an adult, teenagers need to separate themselves from the adults who have previously taken care of them (that's you!) and develop new relationships in the wider community. They must learn to recognize their own needs (and make decisions about how to meet these needs), and become autonomous, independent and self-governing.

Now, I know this isn't news to you. You understand that your teenager is on the road to independence. Indeed, you might well be feeling frustrated at your teen's patchy progress along that road. To your eyes, it might look like your teenager is making no headway at all – they are eating your food, need constant nagging to do anything at all and are firmly ensconced in their bedroom. It probably doesn't look like they are going anywhere right now.

Yet, behind that bedroom door, the work of becoming independent is certainly going on. As parents, we tend to view independence as a destination that teenagers are working toward, but child development doesn't work that way. It's not linear. Children learn through practice and repetition. They get better at things by doing them. And at each stage of their lives, children are driven by strong internal forces to try out the skills they will need for the next stage. For you, becoming independent might be all about your teen doing well at school so they can get into college and start on a good career path. For your teen, independence is what they are living and breathing right now.

Rather than a journey or a destination, it is more helpful to think of a teen's progress toward adulthood in terms of four key drives:

- **Separation** – extracting themselves from the family.
- **Autonomy** – taking control of their own lives and decisions.
- **Individuation** – defining themselves and their unique identity.
- **Assimilation** – learning to fit in as a member of their society.

These four drives are the propellors behind teen behaviour. At each moment, one of these drives will almost certainly be in play, and sometimes all of them. This isn't something your teenager chooses or is in control of – this is the developmental work of adolescence. And, just like that toddler obsessively bouncing up and down to strengthen their legs, your teenager is compelled by these four drives to flex their independence muscles without fully understanding why or what they are doing.

And, just like a toddler learning to walk, your teen's progress won't be neat or linear (and there will definitely be some bruises). Sometimes, it might look like your teen's behaviour is the direct opposite of independence-seeking – but if we dig a little deeper and stand in their shoes, we can usually spot one of their four independence drives at play. For example, a teenager who withdraws to their bedroom might not look like they are flying the nest to face life solo. Yet, by withdrawing to their room they are practising the skills of independence by:

- putting a barrier between themselves and family [*separation*]
- taking control of their own living space and making decisions about what to do in it and how it looks [*autonomy*]
- exploring their identity through clothes, make-up, posters, music [*individuation*]
- messaging with their peer group and practising their social skills [*assimilation*].

A teenager's bedroom is the training ground where they role play independence. And, because humans get better at what we practise, the more your teenager manifests these four developmental drives, the more skilled at independence they will be and the stronger they will become to make the leap into young adulthood.

But what if they are being totally irresponsible? Spending hours in their room staring at a screen instead of studying? That's the opposite of being a responsible young adult! I hear you. Just because your teen is practising their independence skills, doesn't mean they will do so well or responsibly. Sometimes, these four driving forces will come out in behaviour that looks to us like the opposite of increasing maturity – such as exercising their autonomy by leaving uneaten bananas to rot under their bed or staying up late before an exam practising their assimilation skills Snapchatting with mates. When flexing those fledgling independence wings, teens are going to make bad decisions as well as good ones.

These four independence drives won't always come out in obvious or consistent ways. One minute your teen might want nothing to do with you and throw nasty comments your way to keep you at bay [*separation*] and the next minute they might be so overwhelmed by friendship issues [*assimilation*] that they curl themselves up on your bed for comfort and conversation (usually when you are desperate to go to sleep!). Some teens will seem to be moving in the opposite direction to one of these drives. For example, a socially anxious teen might go to great lengths to avoid social situations, but that's not because the need to assimilate with their peer group isn't driving them. On the contrary, it's because their desire to fit in [*assimilation*] is so overwhelming, they are frozen in fear.

I'm not suggesting that as parents we should just excuse how our teen chooses to manifest their independence drives and just leave them to it. But learning to spot these drives in action is incredibly helpful. If we can recognize the forces behind our teen's behaviour, we are much more likely to be able to connect with them and influence their development positively.

ACTION POINT

Before you read on, stop for a minute, and have a think.

- What behaviour are you finding particularly hard at the moment in relation to your teen?
- How might one, or more, of their four developmental drives [*separation, autonomy, individuation, assimilation*] help you understand that behaviour differently?

What's going on inside their brains?

Now, let's get micro and take a look at what's going on inside the teenage brain to translate these four independence drives into thoughts and actions. Teenagers might look nearly grown-up on the outside, but there is still a LOT of neurological building work going on in their brains.

Roughly speaking, the human brain is composed of three main areas.* The back part of the brain governs our instinctive survival functions (such as heart rate and breathing). It is this part of the brain which takes over when there is no time for thought and we need to act quickly – for example, by priming us for evasive action when we are in danger. Then, there is the front part of the brain, which is often referred to as our "thinking" brain. This houses the prefrontal cortex that powers the higher-level executive functions which enable us to do things like planning a sequence of actions to reach a goal. The behaviours governed by these executive

---

* What follows is a high-level overview of brain structure and development condensed to make it accessible. If you want a more detailed explanation, I recommend Frances E. Jensen, *The Teenage Brain* (HarperCollins, 2015).

functions tend to be the behaviours we typically associate with increasing maturity and that we most want to see in our teenagers, such as:

- remembering to do things (without being reminded)
- devising a study schedule (and sticking to it)
- focusing on a task (without being distracted)
- being organized (not losing things)
- staying calm and thinking things through (without getting emotional)
- weighing up decisions carefully (not acting on impulse).

In between the front and back parts of the brain there is the limbic system which governs our emotions. It is here that we find the amygdala which plays a key role in triaging information coming into the brain and directing it either toward the thinking front brain or toward the back brain regions. The amygdala is always on the lookout for threats, scanning information coming in through our senses for signs of danger so these can be sent straight to the back of the brain for an immediate defensive response.

The back regions of the brain are the most critical to our survival as these govern the bodily processes that sustain life. Logically therefore, as children grow, their brain development tends to focus first on securing the crucial back regions before progressing through the limbic areas toward the frontal lobes. Once puberty arrives and children enter adolescence, most of the neurological groundwork in their brains has been completed. The brain shifts its attention to upgrading the speed and accuracy with which signals are transmitted along its networks. This is akin to a major rewiring project which entails insulating the signal wires, pruning out pathways that aren't being used, and installing faster connectors so that the young adult brain will be in top performance mode for the shift to independent living.

However, this final performance upgrade also progresses from back to front, starting in the instinctive back section of the brain and moving forward through the emotional middle brain regions and finishing at the front. This means that the parts of the teenage brain governing emotions are upgraded before their more rational prefrontal cortex gets its turn. In essence, the emotional centre of the teenage brain is firing on all cylinders at a time when the thinking front part is still connected via 3G. With insecure connectivity, the signal from a teen's thinking brain frequently drops out, or is simply drowned out by the louder, clearer signals from their emotional brain regions.

Eventually, once the adolescent brain has finished upgrading (at around 25 years old), the connections between the front and back parts of their brain will form a fully functioning information highway and their thinking brain will be less easily knocked offline (though even adults struggle with this occasionally!). In the meantime, your teenager might seem a bit Jekyll and Hyde: flooded with emotion and utterly unreasonable one moment (while the link to their thinking prefrontal cortex is down) and then back to their best, sweet, rational, thoughtful selves the next (once their emotions have quietened down and the prefrontal cortex is back online).

How teen brains drive teen actions

Are you saying that my teenager's brain is making them behave this way? The fact that teens' limbic regions are all revved up while their prefrontal cortex is still a work in progress goes a long way to explaining typical teen behaviour. The prefrontal cortex plays a crucial role not just in modulating our emotions but also in inhibiting unacceptable behaviour. If your erstwhile well-behaved and compliant child is now slamming doors or being aggressive and generally breaking all the polite behaviour rules you spent ten years teaching them, changes in their brain will be a factor. Without a restraining steer from their prefrontal cortex, teens have much weaker mechanisms holding them back from being rude or lashing out or having a meltdown.

My teen doesn't get emotional and he doesn't shout at me. He just ignores me and won't talk to me at all. Not all teenagers externalize their emotions. While one teenager will spray out their emotions in grand gestures or a loud voice, another teenager might be embroiled in an equally intense internal world while, to the casual observer, it looks like they are just watching YouTube. They might look blank. They might say they don't care. That doesn't mean they aren't full to the brim with big feelings inside. When the brain's limbic system is in full throttle, and a teen can't handle it, shutting down is a common response.

This back to front brain development also makes teenagers much more susceptible to the lure of thrills and rewards. Pleasurable, rewarding feelings are generated via our limbic system, which is all pumped up and full-systems-go in teenagers. But with the front part of their brains less securely in control, teens find it harder to resist temptation. Their full-volume reward signals easily drown out any whispers of caution from the thinking part of their brain, making teens far more likely to act on impulse or to make reward-based decisions (despite their better judgement or, indeed, your sage advice). A teen might struggle to control big dangerous reward impulses (like jumping in the river to impress their friends) or trip up on smaller everyday impulses (such as watching yet another episode of that funny cartoon even though they know there is homework to be done).

My teen hardly leaves their room, they'd never jump off a bridge! The dominance of the limbic system in the teenage brain doesn't always lead to pleasure-seeking or risk-taking. It also makes teens more prone to feeling scared or threatened, and more vulnerable to anxiety. Without a steadying counterbalance from the more reasonable "let's think things through" frontal lobes, a teen's amygdala (which is always on the lookout for threat) can start to see danger in every situation and get trigger-happy on the panic button, sending out wave after wave of fight–flight–freeze signals.

This anxious response sometimes springs from causes parents can easily identify – such as a teen who is so stressed about failing an exam that they can't concentrate in order to study. But often the triggers are less obvious, or they might seem trivial to us, because what a teenager perceives as a threat is different from the threats we worry about as parents. The teenage amygdala is especially quick to perceive threats (real or imaginary) which relate to those four big developmental drives [*separation, autonomy, individuation, assimilation*]. For example, a teenager might react to a loving parent knocking on their door to tell them that dinner is ready as a threat to their right to make their own decisions about what they do when [*autonomy*] and send out an aggressive "Go away!" fight response. Another teen might be so sensitive to the social threat of being left out [*assimilation*] that they will engage in foolish or unkind activities to stay part of the in-crowd. Another might withdraw from friendships altogether and stay at home rather than risk the danger of not being liked. With their limbic systems outranking their thinking brains, teens weigh up risks differently from adults and it can often be hard for us to perceive the real sense of threat driving their response (and all too easy for us to dismiss it as out of proportion).

Of course, all teens are different. Brain development can follow a similar path but proceed at varying rates for each teenager or manifest in different behaviours. Some teens will show signs of maturity earlier. Their stronger executive functions will help them do well in end-of-school exams and keep them steady in their first steps into independence. For neurodivergent teens (for example, those who are autistic or have ADHD), this period can be especially turbulent. The development of their executive functions may take a different trajectory or proceed at a different pace, and they can find it especially hard not to be overwhelmed by a highly reactive threat-adverse amygdala.

None of this is a sign that the adolescent brain isn't working properly. On the contrary, this is your wonderful teenager's brain shifting into the neurological activation patterns that will lead them toward exactly the behaviours they need for this stage of development – behaviours that build their independence skills and operationalize their drive toward *separation*, *autonomy*, *individuation* and *assimilation*. Being drawn toward rewards gives teens a phenomenal ability to learn and impels them to strike out on their own. Being intensely affected by emotions helps teens forge deep bonds with their friends. Being alert to threat helps teens navigate society and find a place within it. This heightened sensitivity comes at exactly the time children need it most – when they are stepping away from the protection of the family unit and taking their place independently in society.

But it doesn't always make it easy to be a teenager. Or, indeed, to live with one.

"Who am I going to be?"

If you are finding it hard to recognize your teenager, believe me, they are struggling even harder to get a handle on who they are. In all likelihood, your child spent their first ten years bobbing along within family life (whatever that looked like) absorbing the habits, values, likes and dislike of your family culture. Family is how children understand themselves. The things we do together and the choices we make as a family unit build children's sense of themselves and where they belong. However, once they enter their teenage years children are plunged into much choppier waters. Suddenly, they need to distance themselves from family [*separation*] and start owning their choices [*autonomy*]. Yet each choice they make says something about them [*individuation*] and has to be considered from the point of view of how it looks and what others might think of them [*assimilation*]. This is a complex juggling act that requires teens to step out from the protective bubble of family and construct a new independent identity.

Where does a teenager find the materials for constructing an identity? Looking around, they have limited options. Most of a teen's life is dictated to them. They can't choose where they live. They have to go to school (whether they like it or not). Travelling around independently can be a challenge, and (as their parents often remind them) this is not their house and they're not paying the bills, so they don't get to make the decisions. One of the few ways a teenager can establish their identity is through their choices – the way they wear their clothes, the style of their hair, the brands they like, their musical tastes, the computer games they play. So, teens use these tools to work out (and mark out) the type of person they are (or they want to be) and to signal what they stand for.

From the outside, this strategy of identity through proxy markers can look less like our teens discovering their authentic selves and more like them trying on costumes off the peg. Your teen might suddenly parrot a whole different language, speaking to their friends in an accent they have never used before, using words you may not like. They might crave a specific brand of clothes which they are adamant are vital to their happiness and use every strategy in their emotional toolbox to leverage these out of you. Many of your teen's identity experiments will be fleeting and superficial (six months later, you'll find that prized designer hoodie crumpled under their bed never to be worn again). Others will reveal a truth about themselves that lasts forever. There is nothing false or inauthentic about this process, each new iteration of identity contains something important your teen is learning about themselves.

As a parent, it can be tricky to keep up with these sudden identity shifts or, indeed, to accept them, especially when they challenge our values or our idea of our child. Having spent over a decade getting to know our child so well, we naturally cling a little to the child version of them we have grown to love so much. We might think we know our child better than they know themselves – when the truth is, they are the ones on the inside working out who they are becoming, and we are on the outside catching up. It takes huge courage for teens to show the world who they are, so never mock or dismiss or reject your teen's self-expression. Whatever identity your teen is exploring, revealing or experimenting with, what they need from us is to let them know wholeheartedly that the person they are is utterly acceptable, lovable and precious.*

Indeed, you will probably notice your teen's confidence and self-esteem tracking their identity shifts. Your teen might oscillate between an arrogant certainty that the current version of themselves is right in every single way and then lurch to crippling self-doubt as their trust in this particular look or personality wanes (or as their friends' preferences suddenly pivot). To us, it might seem like teens have got everything out of proportion and are obsessing about petty points of difference – but in an age when every choice will be scrutinized, these are no trivial matters.

---

* This is especially important when it comes to gender identity and sexuality. LGBTQ+ teens are at higher risk of poor mental health and are more vulnerable to bullying, so being accepting and maintaining a close relationship will be especially important.

ACTION POINT

THE MESSY BEDROOM

Messy teen bedrooms are one of the most common com-plaints I hear from parents. But what if we viewed that untidy room through a different lens? Not as a sign of all the things our teen has failed to do (hang up their clothes, take their dishes downstairs, wipe up that spilled drink, etc) but as a manifestation of how much they have going on in their lives and in their minds?

- Those cosmetics (without lids) strewn in front of the mirror: might these reveal just how hard your teen must be trying to find a path between social expectations and self-belief?
- Those carpet burns from abandoned hair straighteners: might these show how frantic the daily juggle to be camera-ready must feel?
- The dumb-bells gathering dust next to an empty tube of acne cream: how difficult must it be to prioritize when everything is important?

Discarded pen lids, a broken games controller, eyelash curlers next to crumpled notes for an essay on the suffragettes, that motivational sign hanging off the wall (Dream Big! Be Kind! Keep Smiling!), last year's birthday cards . . . when we take time to look, it is awe-inspiring how much our teens are dealing with, how many elements they are trying to reconcile and how much energy that must take.

Take a fresh look. What might you see if you looked at your teen's messy room through different eyes?

"Where do I fit in?"

They just need to be themselves, don't they? What other people think shouldn't be so important to them. These proxy signifiers – clothes, hair, places, hobbies – are so important because teenage identity is never just about working out who they *are*, but also about who they are *seen* to be. The question teens need to answer isn't just "Who am I?" [*individuation*] but also "Where does this 'me' fit in?" [*assimilation*]. At the same time as working out their own views and preferences, teens are benchmarking these on the social approval scale and asking themselves, *What would my friends think if they saw me doing this?* It's almost as if they carry around an imaginary audience* of friends in their mind's eye to check how their thoughts, actions and appearance might be perceived at any moment.

Of course, we all do this to some extent, parents included, but a teen's imaginary audience is especially powerful. We know from experiments using MRI scans that the thought of being observed registers much more strongly in a teenager's brain than in an adult's or a child's, and their stress response is activated when teens believe (or imagine) that another teenager is watching them. Their hearts beat faster, their skin might flush, they start to sweat – just at the thought of being observed by another teenager. Once you throw social media into the mix – and the real prospect that someone actually could be looking at your photo or latest group chat contribution right this instant – then teenage self-consciousness can quickly escalate into anxious overdrive.

As parents, we want our teens to feel good about themselves and to know that they are wonderful and

---

* The term "imaginary audience" was first used by psychologist David Elkind. There is a helpful summary of the research behind this concept in Sarah-Jayne Blakemore's *Inventing Ourselves: The Secret Life of the Teenage Brain* (Black Swan, 2019). If you want details on the research experiments that have helped us understand more about the teenage brain, this would be the best book to read.

lovable just the way they are. We get frustrated when we see them caring so much about what other people think or following the herd and jumping onto a bandwagon. Yet, for your teen, integrating into their peer group isn't a choice. Their brains, bodies and developmental drives are all screaming at them to try and fit in. Psychologists call this fitting-in process "peer group adherence". It is as if teenagers are trying to glue themselves to their peer group. From an evolutionary perspective, this makes perfect sense as fitting in is adaptive (if you are part of the herd, you are much more likely to stay alive and find a mate). Learning to read social signals is an ancient survival mechanism, while being rejected by the herd is an existential threat. And, as we know, when survival instincts are in play, those pumped-up regions toward the back of a teenager's brain switch on. So much so that the teenage brain registers social pain with the same intensity on an MRI scan as an adult brain registers physical pain. Just think about that for a moment. When a teenager feels humiliated or excluded (or even just imagines this might happen), their brains respond in the same way as if they'd been physically hurt. They genuinely do feel that pain more than we do.

And, as it hurts so much, it's not surprising that teens try to avoid the disapproval of their peer group as much as possible. They do this in lots of different ways – for example, by always wearing exactly the same brands as their friends or by going along with the crowd (even when they know it's a bad idea). Others try to dodge disapproval by staying out of the limelight and being noticed as little as possible – never asking a question in class, fading into the background in school corridors or hiding out in their bedrooms at home.

Surely, if my teenager was genuinely that bothered by what people think, he would take more showers and go out more? Just because their peer group is important to them doesn't mean they have lots of friends. Teens are acutely aware of where they rank in the social hierarchy. When approval is hard to come by, and being rejected is felt so keenly, withdrawing from social groups and staying in your room (or confining your social interactions to phones or computer games) is a perfectly reasonable strategy for avoiding rejection and protecting some self-worth. Not caring what you wear, or not showering, these are social strategies too, albeit defensive ones. If you are voluntarily excluding yourself and appearing not to want to be part of the group, you can't be rejected. Even with teenagers who hole up in their rooms completely, the pressure of peer group adherence is still in play. These are the teens who will often get violently upset if they can't be online at a particular time of day playing a specific computer game with their online crew.

Most parents feel it keenly when our teens struggle with issues around fitting in. We desperately want to help. Yet, this is also the time when teens are most likely to shrug off our support and reject our opinions. Even if your teen is finding it hard to work out their identity, those developmental drives mean they still have to signal somehow (to themselves and their imaginary audience) that they are no longer the child they used to be. And one of the simplest ways to assert this no-longer-a-child status is to stop joining in family activities and reject their family's likes and dislikes. Your teen may not have worked out who they are yet but the one thing they do know is that they're definitely not you. Because, frankly, everything about you is just wrong.

Parents, "Keep Out!"

Putting aside what it feels like to be rejected by your teenager (we will come to that in the next chapter, I promise), let's have a think about why teens push us away. Identity formation is certainly part of the picture. Belittling someone else's choices and characteristics can feel like a quick way to stake out your own identity. The teenage drive toward independence is so strong it frequently overrides kindness, empathy and consideration. Teens can be really mean. You might overhear your teen being horribly nasty about one of their friends (in a way they would never do to their face), or spot them being vicious to a younger sibling. They will probably mock all your choices as off-brand – what you are wearing, the words you use, the places you go. If you are lucky, this will be a mild joshing rather than a full-scale assassination. If you are unlucky (or in the habit of checking their phone), you will catch them describing you in far more brutal terms (which can be a gut punch if they are still being polite in person).

When teens say these things, it is seldom what they really think. Sometimes, it's simply an act of social positioning (*if I say this, I will sound cool*). Occasionally, they are trying on an opinion (just like they try on different personas) to see how it sounds out loud. More often than not, it's an expression of how they are feeling or reacting in that moment – a sign that their frontal lobes have gone offline or that their amygdala is in threat-response mode.

Anything that gets in the way of their independence can trigger a teen's threat response – and that includes their own feelings. Teenagers don't stop loving us, they just temporarily lose the ability to tolerate loving us. Behind their go-away demeanour, teens love us deeply and want to feel loved by us, yet those feelings are utterly incompatible with their developmental drive toward separation. Loving you, and receiving your love, is still the most important thing in the world to your teen but when those feelings show up, they are prone to set their neurological alarm bells ringing. Those childlike love feelings need to be pushed out of the way if a teen is going to make progress toward independence. It is precisely because they love you so much and are so attached to you that the act of separating from you can be a bit brutal, or they would never manage it (and you might never let go).

This is a truly deep-seated conflict for our teenagers, and it can lead to lots of jumbled-up emotions and responses. For some teens, the easiest way to handle this contradiction is to stick a "Keep Out" sign on their closed bedroom door and avoid those mixed-up feelings altogether.

There is, of course, another reason why teens hide away, though you might not be so comfortable thinking about it: sex. Sexual thoughts and feelings come crashing in with early adolescence. When sex is on their mind (and, at certain periods, sex can be near-constantly on their minds), the physical presence of parents can be intensely uncomfortable. Sex and parents don't mix. Parents are our first loves. Imagine being a young, heterosexual teenage boy who is not yet in control of his sexual impulses, for whom female bodies have suddenly become the focus of overwhelming eroticism (and who is more than likely seeking out porn when he gets the chance). Imagine being that boy and having to live in close proximity to a female body you have been physically affectionate with all your life, but about whom sexual thoughts are utterly taboo. It is hardly surprising if this is too much internal conflict for a young teen to handle and they decide to shut the door and keep completely away from it all for a while.

Being near parents is deeply problematic precisely because they are bonded to us deeply, but these bonds risk compromising their all-important sense of independence. For many teens, this results in seesawing between closeness and distance. They will cuddle up one moment and shrink from your presence like it's toxic the next. Children's development isn't linear, it progresses through trying things out, practising, then going again. At times, your teen might happily snuggle into their old space in the family and stock up on a bit of the loving treatment they used to revel in as a child. But they won't always ask for or accept that love in straightforward ways. And some teens will withdraw almost completely for what feels like a life-changing period of time.

The good news is that your teen will drift back to you, and to the values and habits you have instilled in them. They will start to make up their own mind about issues without feeling like they need to glue themselves quite so closely to the crowd. And they will find a secure enough sense of themselves to be able to love you and spend time with you again. In the interim, your task is to maintain a relationship with them, and find ways to get around that trigger-happy threat response so you can help them through these vulnerable teenage years.

But, let's be clear, for a parent, this stuff hurts, and you are going to need a massive helping of self-compassion to get you through it.

CHAPTER 2
NAVIGATING THE HURTFUL TEENAGE YEARS

Being a teen is intense and tumultuous. However, they are not the only ones who might be feeling like a hot mess inside. The transition from child to adult is seldom gentle on anyone involved, parents included. There is so much at stake – mental health, college places, future careers – and the implications of getting it wrong feel huge. As parents, we want to make everything right for our children but at this exact moment, when the challenges are so great, we start to lose our magic powers. We can no longer heal their hurts with a kiss or make decisions for them.

This loss of power can be sudden. It might happen at 11 years old or at 13. One day we are carefully picking our way through strewn Lego pieces on their bedroom floor and the next we are tiptoeing through smelly trainers, empty cereal bowls and a jumbled heap of every item of clothing from their wardrobe. There is no chance to go back and say goodbye to the child they were, they've gone.

And, if our newly born teen starts to disregard our rules, we can feel utterly disempowered. The discipline strategies we used when they were younger don't work anymore. We can't send them to their rooms (they are in there anyway). When they become secretive, or lash out or refuse to be guided, it's hard to stay calm and keep a sense of perspective. We get drawn into arguments and patterns of behaviour that don't help, but we can't see an alternative.

Navigating the teenage years is as much about us as parents managing our own emotions and reactions and adapting our parenting, as it is about our teen's trajectory of development. To help them through this transition, we need to be the calm, consistent, non-judgemental rock in their turbulent worlds – even when that is far from how we are feeling.

All the feelings, all at once

The teenage years can shake parents to the core. The suddenness of that change from sweet goofy child to stroppy teen can throw us totally off-kilter. Maybe we thought we were doing a half-decent job at parenting for the last ten years or so – the kids were happy and well-behaved and trying hard at school – and then the teenage years come along, and everything seems to come tumbling down.

Perhaps it's because of the enormity of the risks they face. It can feel like our children's entire lives hang in the balance in these few short years. One wrong turn into drugs or alcohol, or hanging with the wrong crowd, could blight their futures forever. Then there are the dangers that lurk online. We can't see these digital threats but (unlike us) they have a direct line to our teen's attention. We are desperate to shepherd them safely through it all, but our previously compliant child now throws all our advice straight back at us, or simply turns off their ears and ignores us. So, our anxiety grows.

We might feel shame – that our teen has turned out "badly". Or self-blame – that their struggles must be our fault. We look around us and see other teens doing well. We scroll past happy family snaps on social media of other people's teens having dinner with their parents, or out walking with them, sightseeing, smiling – while our own teenager won't spend a microsecond longer with us than is strictly necessary.

And then there is the loss of the child that we have spent a whole decade getting to know. The child who adored us and loved us deeply. They are gone forever, transformed into a bigger, clumsier version. Our company is no longer wanted. We aren't even allowed to hang around this new person for scraps of intimacy. With their friends they might be gregarious, but with us they clam up tight. It is a profound rejection by one of the people we love most in the world and into whom we have poured a lifetime's worth of love and nurturing.

Rejection speaks to the deepest parts of us. It can spark rage, fury, sadness. *How dare they be so ungrateful and disobedient after everything I have done for them and continue to do?* And, as they withdraw, we chase them further into their private spaces to make our point, because we don't feel listened to, we don't feel seen.

We catch glimpses of the amazing young adult they could be, and we urge them to become that person (faster, please). Yet the next moment, we can be blindsided by pride at the wonderful human being they are right now, who may not be same as the version we saw in our heads but who is truly admirable, full of fierce loyalty, facing so many demons but still showing up, still trying. We see how hard it is for them and we feel their pain. And as we watch them struggle, for some of us, our own teenage hurts start to surface too, and our own buried pain comes crowding in on top of theirs.

We get little sympathy from our teenager for these internal struggles. We are the dumping ground for all their feelings, good and bad. Despite everything else going on – elderly parents, money problems, career challenges, relationship issues, the rollercoaster mood swings of menopause and night after night sweating and fretting and feeling like we are getting nowhere – we try and hold it together and do the right thing.

PERSONAL STORY

GRIEVING THE LOSS OF CHILDHOOD

Some days, I miss my teenage son so much it makes me cry. He hasn't gone anywhere. He still lives in my house. I still see him every day.

But he doesn't want to be with me anymore. He doesn't really want to speak to me at all.

I try to do the right things. I give him his space and try to enjoy the little moments of connection. When I venture into his teenage lair (or when he is lured out by the need for food, money or a lift), I do all the things I advise other parents to do. I chat to him – not serious personal stuff that will bring his shutters down, just idle fluff about the day, the football results or something funny I've seen on Facebook.

But I can see him thinking, "Please stop, mum. Just shut up and leave me alone."

I see him ticking off the moments until I will leave or be quiet so he can go back to the important teenage stuff he is doing – like listening to music or Snapchatting or playing some stupid mind-numbing game on his phone.

God, I miss my son.

I've been a mother for 16 years and, one way or another, my life has centred around my children. I have received so much love, enjoyed so much intimacy and invested so much thought into how to help my little ones grow into great adults. And now we are reaching the end of their childhood, I am grieving, lost and sobbing.

I am grieving the loss of that little hand in mine. I am grieving the loss of the little boy who sat on my lap wrapped in my arms. I am grieving the loss of a relationship so unique, so all-consuming.

Because now, there is only one of us in that relationship. And a big, vacated hole.

Most days, I know that we will grow a new relationship when he passes through these tricky teenage years. Rationally, I know I need to step back and just be grateful for the small moments of connection. (I cherish the hugs he still sneaks on me when I am not asking for them.) Most days, I know that another precious connection will replace the one we have lost.

But some days, I have absolutely no idea who he is any more. And I am scared that I will never again see the love light up his face when he looks at me.

And, today, that has completely undone me.

The thoughts that trip us up

These are powerful feelings. They don't spring from nowhere. On the face of it, it might seem like it is our teen who is causing these big waves of loss and anger. But when we inspect a little closer, and we are truly honest with ourselves, we can often trace these feelings back to our own thoughts and beliefs. If we want to manage the powerful feelings that come with being the parent of a teenager (so we can be their rock, not add to their storm), we need to examine the internal dialogues and thought patterns that underpin our big feelings.

It can be hard to identify our own thought triggers. Often our reactions come crashing in before we've even noticed our thoughts. In general, there are six common thinking traps that parents of teens typically fall into. Have a read through the list below and see if any of them strike a chord. (Remember, no one is judging you here. Personally, I have fallen into every one of these thinking traps at some time or other, but you might have just one firm favourite that you indulge in a lot.) I call these thought patterns "traps" because they are easy to fall into, harder to get out of and they tend to fuel unhelpful dynamics.

Overgeneralizing

The Overgeneralizing trap is when we reach a negative conclusion based on just one incident. For example, imagine your teen comes home after school and mentions an alter-cation with one of their friends. You start to worry that they are unhappy at school, or that they might be being bullied (but not telling you about it), or that they are struggling to make friends and becoming socially isolated. You globalize a negative conclusion from one piece of evidence. This particular thinking trap is often accompanied by a sense of panic that it all seems to be going wrong.

Catastrophic Thinking

The Catastrophic Thinking trap is similar to overgeneralizing, but it tends to involve worrying way into the future. For example, maybe you find out that your 15-year-old has been drinking alcohol in the park with their friends. You start to worry that that they will get addicted to booze or move on to other mind-altering substances, that they will flunk school and end up never getting a decent job and their lives will be blighted by addiction. You get onto a train of worry heading way into the future and feel the whole weight of that imagined future crashing in on the present moment, all because of a couple of beers.

Parents are especially prone to this thinking trap when we identify additional factors which seem to add weight to our catastrophic thoughts. For example, if you find out that your teen has been drinking alcohol and they have ADHD, or they are already struggling to control their impulses, or where there is a family history of addiction, or maybe you just know someone who started drinking as a teenager and ended up never doing well in life, these extra factors all pile up and it can start to feel like you only have a brief window left to save your 15-year-old from a terrible destiny.

Should/Shouldn't

Parents can fall into the Should/Shouldn't trap at any stage of parenting, but it is especially common in the teenage years. It usually happens when our expectations are not met. These might be expectations of our child – for example: *My teenager should know better by now, they're 14 years old, they should be able to remember simple instructions.* Or it might be expectations about your own parenting: *I should be able to get my teenager to listen to me.*

Because teenagers can look so grown-up on the outside (and we have already invested over a decade teaching them how to behave), we often have quite adult expectations of them. When they fail to meet these (for all the reasons outlined in the previous chapter), it can feel like an acute judgement on our parenting. And when other teens seem to be meeting those expectations all around us, it can feel as if our teen's whole character is at stake here. That by failing to load the dishwasher (again) they are revealing themselves to be fundamentally lazy or thoughtless or unkind – rather than just a still-developing young person whose mind is on other priorities and who gets things wrong.

Mind Reading

When we are stuck in the Mind-Reading trap, we assume we know what is going on in our teen's mind without asking them. For example, you might worry that your teenager is upset by a friendship issue when actually they aren't bothered by it. Or you assume they are shouting at you because they are being disrespectful when, in fact, something has happened at school that day which has really shaken them.

Comparisonitis

The Comparisonitis trap. We've all done it. Watched another teenager hug their parents goodbye as they head off on a school trip while ours won't even make eye contact. Or scrolled through social media comparing our underperforming reality to the picture-perfect lives we find showcased there. We see other people's teens being lauded for sporting achievements, altruism or musical talents, alongside smug parental boasts about academic achievements – while our own teenager spends all their free time gaming or watching make-up tutorials and dashes off their homework in the shortest time possible. Even holiday snaps of teens looking like they are enjoying themselves can land like a gut punch. *Why is my teenager not doing that? What's wrong with them? What did I do wrong?*

If your teen is truly struggling with their self-esteem or mental health, even simple everyday events like turning up to watch a sports match knowing that your teen is at home because they couldn't face it (while all these other teens are here smiling and laughing) can set off heart-breaking comparisons.

It's All About Me!

As modern parents we love to think that we're incredibly important. We love to take the credit for our kids' successes (and we heap the blame on ourselves when things don't go well). We want our efforts to be recognized and appreciated, which, when it comes to teenagers, is a bit of a problem. Not that you don't deserve to be appreciated – you absolutely do – you're just barking up the wrong tree expecting appreciation from a teenager. Teens are deeply self-absorbed (for all the reasons we saw in the last chapter!) and trying to separate from you and become independent means never acknowledging that they couldn't have managed something on their own without you.

Teens tend to talk in absolutes (*I hate you! You always make me feel bad! You never let me do it my way!*). Generally, they are simply reaching for big words to convey big feelings or are trying to communicate that an issue is really important to them. However, when parents are stuck in the It's All About Me! trap, we tend to hear these big words as blame or attack rather than as a plea for understanding. The truth is this really isn't about you. This is a developmental process your teenager is going through. Some teens are easy, some are difficult, some have an easy ride, some have it hard – and it's not necessarily a result of your parenting. There will be impacts on you, for sure, and these might be difficult to cope with but when you make it all about you – your emotions, your fears, your expectations – it's much harder to hear what your teen is saying or to look behind their behaviour and see what's driving it or how you might help them move forward.

The cycles parents get stuck in

If you read through those six thinking traps and recognized every single one of them, that's great. Seriously, brilliant! It would be totally unrealistic to avoid all these traps completely. This isn't about judging yourself or rating your parenting. It's about identifying which of your thought patterns are helpful and which are unhelpful, which of your thoughts fuel positive interactions and which ones generate conflict and hurt. These six common thinking traps tend to activate parents' fears and deepest emotions, and they frequently lead us to make poor choices in how we interact with our teen, so it's really important to learn to spot them.

But my teenager IS being ungrateful, they shouldn't treat me like that. And drugs ARE dangerous! I'm not arguing that these thoughts are untrue, just that they are unhelpful. Indeed, it is precisely because they are often grounded in a kernel of reality that these thinking traps can be so triggering. The dangers modern teens face are real, but catastrophic thoughts about our teenager's life being ruined by one of these dangers don't tend to lead us toward helpful actions. For example, a head full of thoughts about all the dangers lurking on the internet* is more likely to send you hurtling into an ineffective lecture (to be greeted with huffs and eyerolls) rather than a helpful conversation that will equip your teen with the knowledge and skills to manage their online safety sensibly.

When we as parents get stuck in thinking traps, our emotional alarm buttons are repeatedly activated. Our emotional brains take over and we get sucked into negative interactions that fail to improve the situation in any way but succeed in driving a wedge between us and our teenager. In short, we end up ranting but nothing changes.

> *What happened? You were supposed to load the dishwasher? I'm really tired of this, you do nothing around the house. How are you ever going to hold down a job if you can't remember to do simple things? You just don't care about other people, do you? I work hard all day to keep a roof over our heads, and this is how you repay me. You are old enough to know better. Your sister was cleaning the whole house at your age.*

Can you spot the thinking traps?† Teenagers not helping out around the house is incredibly frustrating, for sure, and

---

* Porn, drugs, groomers, gambling, self-harm messaging, fraudsters – to name just a few.

† *What happened? You were supposed to load the dishwasher? I'm really tired of this – you do nothing around the house* [**overgeneralizing**]. *How are you ever going to hold down a job if you can't remember to do simple things* [**catastrophizing**]? *You just don't care about other people, do you* [**mind-reading**]? *I work hard all day to keep a roof over our heads, and this is how you repay me* [**it's all about me**]. *You are old enough to know better* [**should/shouldn't trap**]. *Your sister was cleaning the whole house at your age* [**comparisonitis**].

you are right to want to tackle it. But when we give vent to negative thoughts, we usually just end up even more frustrated. We shout, nothing changes. We shout louder, nothing changes. We reach for consequences, these don't work. So, we up the stakes. *You won't listen to me? Then I will take your phone away for a whole week!* We fight to maintain some control over our independence-seeking teenager but end up losing it anyway and drain all the goodwill from our relationship. Leaving our teen even less likely to listen to us next time.

The cycle of negative interactions

Each time we go around the cycle our relationship with our teenager seems to slide further away. When we are feeling negative about our teens, you can be sure that our teens detect that. When we write them off in our catastrophic statements (*You're never going to pass your exams at this rate!*), they hear us, and it hurts. Our opinion really matters to them. And when they are already struggling to believe in themselves, knowing that we think they are getting it all wrong makes them a lot less inclined to give us airtime. They might even decide to live up to the negative future we have assigned to them.

Worries and negative thoughts are inevitable when you are the parent of a teenager. Our job is to learn to spot those thoughts (underneath the big emotions they generate), take a deep breath and try out a different thought instead. Not to dump those thoughts and fears onto our teenager or hijack the drama. That's easy to say but not so easy to do. You will make mistakes as you learn, and that's OK. Just try to notice those mistakes and do them a little less often.

PERSONAL STORY

THE ONE WHERE I FORGOT TO BE THE GROWN-UP AND GOT IT ALL WRONG (FROM THE PHONE ARCHIVES)

I don't know why you love to constantly make me feel like shit Mum. I did absolutely nothing wrong just then and it resulted in you shouting at me and then crying. I come down to apologize (even though I haven't done anything) and you are still being rude to me.

I have had enough of your anger, I can't absorb any more of it. You are not the only one who has big emotions. Grow up and be a bit kinder.

What are you on about Mum, what are you actually on about? I was offering to pay for the cinema by doing jobs for you and for some reason you just started being rude and acting like I'm a piece of shit saying I won't do the jobs and just speaking to me like I'm a no one. Do you know how that makes me feel. And then I went into my room before I got angry and you just came in to my room shouting.

Even if you don't see everything I do for you or value it, you could at least pretend to be grateful just because that would make me feel better.

I am grateful, I don't understand what to do to show I'm grateful Mum I'm only 16.

Five Golden Rules for parents of teens

How on earth am I supposed to avoid all those traps, control my feelings and get it right? Especially when my teen barely talks to me anyway! The teenage years have a reputation for being difficult for good reason. This is a whole new Jedi level of parenting.* To succeed, you will need to scale new heights of calm, empathy and self-regulation. And the onus will

---

* I came across the phrase "Jedi parenting" in Lorraine Candy's book *Mum, What's Wrong With You? 101 Things Only Mothers of Teenage Girls Know* (4th Estate, 2021). The phrase captures perfectly the depths of inner calm and wisdom parents of teens need to draw upon!

be firmly on you to adapt your parenting to your changing child's needs. I'm not saying it's going to be easy. It might be smooth, or it might be rocky. If you can try to follow these Five Golden Rules, they will ease your path and ensure you come out the other side with a good relationship with your young adult offspring.

1 Be kind to yourself

Most of us derive a huge amount of self-worth and sense of purpose from our parental roles. When teens start to push us away, it's a big hit. You might feel old, a bit lost, unsure of who you are anymore now the kids are growing up. When we have shared so much love and time with our children, separating from them – losing them – can be brutal. It's OK to have those feelings. These feelings will lessen with time and eventually pass.

In the meantime, it's essential you take responsibility for your side of this transition and hold yourself accountable for your own happiness. If you don't, you will be buffeted by the winds of your teenager's ups and downs. This is the time for self-compassion. Be kind to yourself. Look after yourself, physically and mentally. Manage your own wellbeing actively and go looking for some joy. Because this is also the time for reinvention, for discovering who this new post-children "you" might become. Explore new passions, try out new hobbies, reconnect with friends and find ways to enjoy life, lighten the load and laugh (lots). Your teen might still be really difficult when you come home but you will be re-energized to go again. And, most importantly, you'll be supporting their separation process by doing your half of that developmental work.

2 Manage your thoughts (to manage your feelings)

If you want to stay calm and respond thoughtfully, you will need to manage your emotions. And that means learning to catch your thoughts and challenging them. If you are reacting emotionally, or you are fretting about your teen, pay close attention to the words you are using inside your head. Can you spot a thinking trap? For example, if your teen's results at school are dipping, you might be saying to yourself that they are failing because they don't try hard enough, that they're lazy, or that they don't understand the importance of doing well at school. Perhaps you're thinking that if they don't do well at school now, that will impact on the rest of their lives? Now notice your body. What physical sensations have these thoughts lead to? Is your heart racing? Your head pounding? Do you feel a sense of pressure to do something? What actions might these thoughts and sensations lead to? A shouting match? Confiscating their digital device? Sleepless nights?

Now, pause, take a deep breath and imagine you are a different parent (not you). What alternative thoughts might another parent have in these circumstances? For example, another parent in the same situation could think: *I wonder what's going on with them that's getting in the way of studying?* Or: *School doesn't really interest them.* If you were to have these alternative thoughts, how would your body be feeling? What alternative actions might these alternative thoughts lead you toward?

Learning to catch and challenge our own thoughts helps us to get some perspective and to remember that it is not our teenager that is provoking our emotional reaction, it's our own beliefs about that situation. By learning to think flexibly and examine the situation from different viewpoints, we can learn to reflect before acting and be calmer and more thoughtful in approaching our teen.

3 Model the behaviour you want to see

I don't know about you but when I'm confronted with a teenager whose thinking brain has been hijacked by their emotions, my hackles tend to rise and my emotional temperature shoots up. If I'm not careful, my own thinking brain goes offline too, and we're left with two out-of-control amygdalae reacting off each other.

There is nothing wrong with feeling angry, upset or infuriated with your teen. You are human, not a saint. But rather than descending into that primitive emotional brain space, try to model to your teenager how it is possible to manage big feelings well. Walk away. Say: *I'm too angry to speak with you right now, I'm going to go and calm down.* Light the path and show them how it's done. I use a mantra to remind myself of this in the heat of the moment. My mantra is "Be the grown-up" – but use whatever phrase works for you!

If you don't like the relationship you have with your teenager right now, model the relationship you want to have with them. Occupy the space you want them to join you in. Speak politely and respectfully. Be kind to them through small thoughtful gestures. These gestures won't always be appreciated (or even noticed) and sometimes they will be batted straight back at you with an added helping of scorn. Be the grown-up, let the failures pass, be forgiving. Model to your teen how to see the world from someone else's point of view and how to compromise. When you get it wrong, say sorry and repair. Be the adult you want them to become.

4 Hand over the power

Always remember what's driving your teen's behaviour. The teenage developmental project is all about independence. And that means it's all about power. You've got the power, they want it. They want control over themselves and their lives – whether you think they're ready for it or not. If you hang back, or drag your feet, or cling on to power, your teen will go ahead and make their own decisions and seize that power in spite of you. The drive for *separation*, *autonomy*, *individuation* and *assimilation* is going to happen with or without you.

A natural response to losing authority is to try and assert it even more strongly. To lay down the rules, confiscate the phone, come down hard and jump on every single scrap of disobedience or poor judgement. But if you try to impose your power through force of will, there is going to be conflict and damage. Some teens are wonderfully responsible and take on new freedoms sensibly. Others are risk-takers or full of fears, or just forgetful and easily led astray. Whichever yours is, you will still need to find ways to hand over power positively and allow them to make mistakes.

If you can show willing and be an active participant in this handover of power, you are much more likely to be able to avoid conflict, maintain a good relationship, and draw boundaries around the really important issues. If you can, try to introduce freedoms in small manageable steps. But remember, even little steps will feel scary to you (it's not a real compromise if it's not a little uncomfortable). This is a chicken-and-egg situation. By handing over some power, we signal to our teen that we believe they are capable of being responsible. By having some power, our teen learns to be capable of that responsibility.

5 Prioritize relationship over principle

You may not have absolute control over your teen any longer, but you do have influence. And the better your relationship with your teenager, the more you will be able to influence their choices positively. So, always prioritize relationship over standing on principles. Easy to say, I know, not so easy to do when your teen is spouting clever-dick comments at you or doing the exact opposite of what you've asked. Faced with a stubborn, withdrawn or recalcitrant teen, our overwhelming urge is to pull them up, go head-to-head and force them to admit they are wrong – all at the price of precious goodwill that will not be easy to win back.

Prioritizing a positive relationship over standing on principle is not a sign of lax parenting. It's probably the best hope we have of getting through this transfer of power in a relatively peaceful manner. Don't blow all your parental capital on micromanaging the small stuff or picking fights over a sarcastic attitude. Let it go. Keep on loving them (and showing them that you love them) despite their mistakes and they will know they are lovable even at their worst. And you will still have their ear when it matters and a much better platform for nudging them toward good decisions.

When it comes to the teenage years, relationship really matters. So, how do you build a relationship with a teenager who wants nothing to do with you? Well, that's the subject of our next chapter. . .

CHAPTER 3

PERSUADING A RELUCTANT TEEN TO SPEND TIME WITH YOU

Teenagers are vulnerable on many fronts; they have difficult stuff to deal with inside and out. The best plan for supporting them safely into young adulthood is to stay close and walk alongside them on their journey through these tricky years. However, maintaining a good relationship with a teenager who has withdrawn from family life is not easily done. Relationships thrive on trust, communication, goodwill and spending time together – all of which can be in short supply between teens and their parents. A teen in withdrawal mode is prepared to put a lot of effort into avoiding being close to their parents. Right now, it probably feels like you are the only one still in this relationship (or you might be feeling so battered that you'd rather steer clear and avoid any more barbs).

If you want to build a relationship with your teen, you need to be realistic. This isn't about insisting that they spend a specific number of hours with you (there is no simple equation that X hours of family time = a happy teenager). There is no point reaching for the stars and expecting good humour and a consistent connection with them. When it comes to teenagers, connection (and good humour!) tends to happen in fleeting moments that we can't predict or control.

Perhaps a more reasonable goal is simply to keep holding open the space they have vacated in their relationship with you. To be gently, doggedly there. Still available, still liking them and happy to spend time with them. Not giving up on them despite their rejection and withdrawal. If you can find a way to go through the motions of your relationship with your teen as if they are in it with you – the rituals, the gestures, the kindnesses and compromising – and not be put off no matter how hard they try to push you away or how often they refuse to join in, then you're on the right path. We can't make teens want to spend time with us. But we can model the relationship we want to construct with this newly independent young person and leave a trail of breadcrumbs toward our warmth, support and connection for whenever they are ready for it.

There's no question you'll need heaps of patience and Olympian levels of self-restraint for all this – this is Jedi parenting, indeed! Your mission is to build a relationship, but that is 100 percent not your teen's priority. Your teen is busy trying to get out of their relationship with you [*separation*]. With those four independence drives firing on all cylinders, even just the physical presence of a parent can be a source of discomfort for teenagers. Spending time with us isn't a simple matter for them, it involves many layers of jeopardy. There is the risk they might miss out on a vital digital interaction that endangers their peer group adherence. There is the fear of being seen with their parents, by someone who matters. And even if they stay hidden at home with us, there is the issue of what their internal imaginary audience of friends might think.

With all those conflicts going off inside, there is little point insisting that that your teen slips back into the space their child-self used to occupy in your family activities. If we want to tempt a teen out of their bedroom, we have to find ways of spending time with them that helps them step around their conflicted feelings. And we need to avoid getting in the way of their real job of constructing their young adult selves. We need to point forward to a new relationship in which they are loved and secure but no longer a child.

Persuading a reluctant teen to spend time with you is all about compromise, patience and oh-so-softly catching their best moments.

"You're coming whether you like it or not!"

However, before you get to that point, there's a pretty good chance you'll take a detour via the "You're coming whether you like it or not!" strategy. Most parents of disengaged teens try this approach at some point or other. Our natural response to waning authority is to try and assert it even more forcefully and leverage every last ounce of parental control to insist that our teenager joins in.

The problem with this approach is that if your teen is absolutely dead set on not engaging (rather than just a little grouchy), then you're laying the ground for a whole heap of conflict and unpleasantness. Remember, independence is all about power: you've got it, your teenager wants it [*autonomy*]. Trying to force them to do something they don't want to do sets up an oppositional dynamic. For a teenager who is hell bent on declaring their independence, this leaves only one possible power play:

Parent: *Do it!*
Teen: *No!*

The only route they have for protesting their right to choose is to push back at you. So, even if you succeed in forcing a disgruntled teen to come along to granny's or to the theme park or to your best friend's wedding, there's a good chance they will just keep on asserting their non-cooperation in whatever ways they can, and sabotage your attempts at happy family time by scowling, not talking to anyone and badgering you constantly to go home.

If you are stuck in the "You're coming whether you like it or not!" trap, it's worth asking yourself some straight questions. Why does it matter to you so much that they come along?

- Is this really about what other people might think?
- Will it feel like a judgement on you if they don't come?
- Are you drawing conclusions about your teenager from their refusal? (After all, they must be a pretty heartless and ungrateful so-and-so not to want to see their grandmother, right?!)

If any of your answers contain the words "ought to" then the chances are you have succumbed to a thinking trap (probably the Should/Shouldn't trap with a dose of Comparisonitis or Catastrophic Thinking on the side). In which case, this isn't really about building a relationship, is it? This is about you. This is about mustering all your forces to insist your teen comes along because, deep down, you believe that "good" parents have teenagers who want to spend time with them. (They don't – good parents have every type of teenager you can imagine!)

Maybe you are trying to make them come along because you think it will be good for them? Because you think they need the exercise or the fresh air? You may well be right. But by trying to force this one action through, despite resistance, there's a good chance you'll make them even more entrenched in their opposition and less inclined to heed your views about healthy living in the future. Or are you trying to drag them along against their wishes in the hope that if you can just get them there, they will drop the glowering teenager act and enjoy themselves? After all, they used to love bouncing about.

If I can only get her onto the trampoline again, I'll see that innocent joy and love light up her face once more!

I'm sorry, but it isn't going to work, not if they are dead set against it. It doesn't matter how good for them it would be or how much they used to like trampolining, or camping, or your friends Nick and Jo, forging a new independent identity means making their own choices and rejecting the things they liked as a child, at least temporarily. They may well grow up into a young adult who loves spending the night in a tent (indeed, research consistently shows that adults return to many of the activities we enjoyed as children!), but, right now, you are battling against the tide.

If we want to build a relationship with this newly formed teenager in front of us, we need to stop treating them as if they are still the child we used to know, or we risk alienating them further. Step into their shoes. How would you feel if somebody made you do something on the grounds that your wishes are unimportant and your views invalid? Or told you that you will enjoy something when you are absolutely adamant that you won't? Would you feel that this person understood you and was on your side? The teenager in front of you is not the child who loved playing in the woods and paddling in streams. This is a new person, someone you need to get to know, and who needs to get to know themselves and work out what it is that they do and don't like now.

Standing firm in an oppositional dynamic with a teenager tends to drive a wedge and create conflict rather than improve the relationship. And, with a teenager whose emotions are in the neurological driving seat and whose behaviour is under-moderated by the guiding hand of frontal lobes, small conflicts can quickly escalate to real hurt and damage. Standing one's ground and insisting that they do/don't do something is a page from the parenting playbook that's best reserved for really important issues, the ones that threaten our teenager's health and wellbeing, rather than whether they will or won't be coming to Nick and Jo's 25th wedding anniversary.

PERSONAL STORY

THE BARBECUE FROM HELL

The barbecue should have been a simple stress-free affair. A sports club end-of-season gathering. There would be sausages, fizzy drinks, lots of boys of a similar age with plenty of space to run around. What was there not to like?

Except it wasn't my youngest son's sports club, it was his brother's. And he really *really* didn't want to go.

I wasn't having any of it. My dad was visiting, and I had my heart set on a fun family night out. My friends would be at the barbecue with their kids, and I wanted us to be seen – by them, by my dad, by me – as a happy family. In my mind's eye, I was remembering barbecues when the kids were little, and they ran around having the best night ever while the grown-ups drank wine and remembered how to have social lives.

In hindsight, I should have negotiated a compromise, or just left him at home, because he really *really* didn't want to come. Instead, I made the mistake of digging in my heels. I told the grumpy teen that he was coming whether he liked it or not.

The result was a long way from the idyllic family time I had in mind. My 13-year-old set out (with admirable single-mindedness) to sabotage the entire evening by sitting right next to me with his head laid flat on the table. He pointedly ignored every single person who spoke to him (friends, family and strangers) in a determined, silent protest.

My dad was shocked, I was mortified and everyone around us was thoroughly embarrassed.

Looking back, I can see now why he didn't want to be there. I was looking at the barbecue through the lens of childhood not teenagerdom. What my 13-year-old saw was an avalanche of threats:

- boys who weren't his friends, who were a bit older and whose social rules he didn't know
- the possibility that the "wrong" boys from his peer group would be there (who either weren't cool enough to be seen with or who were too cool to be nice to him)
- a mum who would draw attention to him by making him say hello to her friends or inadvertently humiliate him with a display of affection
- being asked questions about himself by unfamiliar adults
- knowing that he carried the weight of a whole heap of family expectations that he didn't understand but almost certainly couldn't meet.

He did the only thing he could, he completely shut down. And I ended the night in tears.

Planning together for family time

I am not suggesting that you abandon the idea of including your teen in family time altogether. Teens may act as if they don't want anything to do with us, but the sense of belonging and security that family provides is an important safety rope in their turbulent worlds. They need to know that family is still there (even if they don't want it) and that they are loved and welcomed (no matter how much they push us away). Yes, we should take account of the message writ large on that closed bedroom door (*"Stay away, I'm not a child anymore!"*) but it doesn't mean we have to blindly obey it.

You are much more likely to succeed in convincing a teenager to come out of their room if you provide choices, and approach things in a spirit of collaboration and compromise. Ideally, we want to avoid going head-to-head with a teen's emotionally reactive subcortical brain regions and engage with their more reasonable frontal lobes instead. And one of the best ways we can do this is to treat our teenagers as if they are already the mature independent young adults that they are fighting to be.

If there is a family event coming up that is likely to cause conflict, don't just spring it on your teen and cross your fingers. Broach it early. Signal upfront your recognition that they – reasonably – might not feel as thrilled about this family occasion as you do. By pre-emptively putting their opposition into words, we reduce the need for them to assert it through their behaviour, and there is a greater chance of staying anchored in discussion. If we can also reduce the potential threat level this upcoming event poses, by signalling our teen's power to make choices, we may be able to stay under the radar of their amygdala's overactive fight-or-flight response. For example, you could say:

> It's Grandma's birthday next month and she's planning a family get together at her house. I appreciate that's probably not your ideal way to spend a weekend. But Grandma thinks the world of you and it would be great to work out a way that you could participate so she knows you're thinking about her. Will you have a think about it and see if you can come up with any ideas that might work for both you and her?

By introducing the problem and leaving them to think about it, you may be able to circumnavigate an emotional or defensive response. If there are any fixed points or issues over which you can't compromise (due to safety, for example), make these clear but present them in the same spirit of collaborative problem-solving.

I'm not willing for you to stay here the whole time because we will be gone overnight but I'm happy to consider other ideas. I'd like us to find a compromise that works for everyone.

Now, just because you are appealing to the thinking part of their brain and treating them with respect, does not mean they will necessarily reciprocate, and there is no guarantee that you won't still end up in conflict. The late development of the prefrontal cortex in adolescent brains can make tasks that involve planning, decision-making and organising much more challenging for a teenager than for an adult, but that doesn't mean you shouldn't persevere. Practising a task strengthens the neural networks required for that task. By treating them as the reasonable and independent decision-makers we want them to become, we are doing what psychologist Dr Adam Price calls "parenting forward"[*] and providing what educationalists refer to as a "scaffold", an external framework that supports an unstable structure while it is being constructed inside.

Try to remain the grown-up prefrontal cortex in the room and keep modelling the process, even if your teenager tries to sabotage the conversation. Accept any idea they offer and allow it on the table for consideration.

My idea is you could just back off, leave me alone and let me get on with my life!

Yes, I can see how you might prefer that. But I don't see how it would help us find a solution that works for both you and for Grandma. So, we'd better look for a compromise.

---

[*] Dr Adam Price, *He's Not Lazy: Empowering Your Son to Believe in Himself* (Sterling, 2017).

Even if they come up with an idea that strikes you as an obvious no-go, treat it with respect. Remember, that adolescent brain is constantly scanning for threats to their autonomy and if you bat their suggestions away, their neurological alarm will go off.

> So, your proposal is to stay here and have Sam over for a sleepover? Well, I can see how that would work for you, but I am not clear how you would be able to make Grandma happy if you did that? Also, it wouldn't meet my need to know that you are safe. I'm pretty sure there is a compromise in there somewhere, but we'll need to work on that idea, so it meets all three criteria.

Don't trivialize their objections, especially if these relate to things they want to do with their friends. To you, it might seem like they spend every second of the day communicating with their friends (and all you are asking them for is a couple of hours!) but for a teen, FOMO (fear of missing out) is one of the biggest threats of all. Even the anticipation that they might miss out on something that they don't yet know about can set their neurological bells ringing and derail discussion. Keep the focus firmly on coming up with solutions rather than getting dragged into a debate about the validity of their objections.

With a reticent teen, you might have to put your own ideas into the mix to lead the way. These ideas will probably be rejected (as they came from you) so don't lead with your best card! And, with a teen who is reluctant to engage, you might have to use the discomfort of your presence to overcome stonewalling and gently press the issue.

> I know you don't want me to be in here, I'm disturbing you. But we need to come up with an idea for Grandma's birthday weekend so we can make plans. I can stay here right now, and we can talk it through, or we can agree a time to talk it through after dinner.

This collaborative problem-solving approach won't work every time. You will need to stay calm, be patient and show that you are willing to compromise (and remember, if it isn't challenging your comfort zone, you aren't really compromising). It may not even result in you spending time with your teen on this occasion. But don't forget our longer-term goal. Our goal is to hold open a kind and supportive relationship and invite them into it. Collaborative planning with your teen isn't just about a specific event, it's a relationship-building act in itself. We are positioning them as independent young adults and making a bid to connect with them in a joint endeavour.

If things get heated, or you can't stay calm, walk away. Don't be tempted to push through if the conversation goes off the rails. If the wrong part of their brain (or yours!) is in the driving seat and they shoot into full battle mode, or if you find yourself enraged by their refusal to engage, take a breath and walk away. Try again another time. Just because it fails once, doesn't mean it will always fail. Keep practising. If you can take their suggestions seriously and show yourself respectful of their views, you will be setting the tone for a new relationship. You'll also be developing a template for solution-focused frontal-lobe-oriented conversations which will come in really handy for tackling lots of other hiccups in these tricky teenage years!

Make allowances (do it their way!)

It's probably going to take more than just their attendance at Grandma's birthday to keep your relationship with your teen strong. A bit of one-to-one time can make a huge difference in keeping you in touch and reminding your teen that you are on their side. When teens withdraw to their bedrooms, they often ditch their old hobbies so we want to do everything we can to prevent teenagers' worlds narrowing too much. The things that they do at this age – hobbies, nutrition, exercise, outings – all contribute to shaping their brains and their futures.

Trying to arrange one-to-one time with a teenager is a bit like trying to spend time with an incredibly awkward friend. That friend who doesn't like trains but who won't drive after dark, who only eats chicken (but not in a sauce), who can't leave the house before 11am, and will cancel at the last minute if it's raining or there's football on. There's little point pushing against the grain if you ever want to see them.

There's no reason why you can't use the collaborative approach to planning some one-to-one time with a reluctant teenager.

> It's half term next week. I know spending time with me is not high on your agenda, but I'd really like it if we could do one thing together. It's your choice what we do. We can do a big thing, like go to the Mall for some shopping or maybe have a spa day? Or we can do something smaller, like taking the dog for a walk or watching a film? It's up to you what we do but I'd really like us to do one thing together. Will you have a think about it and come up with some ideas. I've got lots of ideas, but you'll probably prefer we do one of yours!

However, you might find a "Do you fancy going to the cinema this evening?" approach works better with your particular teen.

Whichever tack you take, flexibility and reasonable expectations will be key. For every ten bids you make for a teen's time, you can expect to get knocked back nine times. Even when they agree to spend time with you, there's a high probability they will cancel or try to wriggle out of it at the last minute. Be as accommodating as you can be. Try to create as many bridges as possible to a positive relationship. The chances of you enjoying time with your teenager (and of them being willing to repeat the experience) will be much greater if you are flexible and work around their needs and interests. That might mean setting off a bit later, stopping for breakfast on route and not lingering as long as you'd like once you're there. It might mean visiting a flagship computer game shop rather than an art gallery and opting for a drive-through lunch rather than the healthier restaurant you'd been hoping for. It might mean ignoring a whole heap of infuriating behaviour. There's a pretty good chance they will forget something important (despite all your reminders) or leave it on a bench. They might even insist on staying three steps away from you at all times. They will almost certainly show less gratitude than you deserve and might well spend the entire time looking as though they aren't enjoying themselves in the slightest.

Your job is to maintain equanimity, focus on the positives and keep the wheels of this relationship turning. Teens in withdrawal mode often don't show much approval or enthusiasm. If it helps, think of that disapproving demeanour as a coat of armour. The concept that being with you might make them happy presents a huge internal conflict to a teen who is bidding for *separation*. Appearing grumpy or aloof on the surface is a neat psychological trick that helps them circumnavigate that conflict and tag along nonetheless. And that's what we need to happen. That disengaged demeanour doesn't necessarily mean that they are not enjoying themselves (though it might impact on your enjoyment if you let it get under your skin!). Returning from a holiday on which he had been unrelentingly negative and had refused to sit at the same table with us for dinner several times, I overheard my son waxing lyrical to his friends via his games console about the amazing beach, pool, food and sightseeing. He regularly refers to it as his best ever holiday (while I still think of it as the holiday that almost broke the maternal camel's back!).

Try not to let any negative behaviour suck you into the Should/Shouldn't trap. Set aside your own sense of outrage and search out the small rewards among the sullenness and eyerolling (just let those go). Remember, spending one-to-one time with a teenager is about reminding them that you are still there, still caring and saving their place in this relationship for them. If you can be flexible and go with their flow in order to oil the wheels of your time together, you are far more likely to stumble upon the little bridges that do lead to connection. Yes, they may have moaned the whole time walking up that hill. They may have complained about the weather, or their shoes, or having to be there at all. But that one moment when you stand looking at the view from the top of the hill and they huddle up to you to shield themselves from the wind and tolerate a cuddle – that's the moment to put in your pocket and treasure. That's the moment to replay in your head and squeeze all you can out of, that one moment of closeness that says *I know you're still here for me*. Those are the moments that matter.

Small moments matter most

In the end, relationships are built from moments, not from perfect day trips. It's the small moments of interaction that form the fabric of a relationship. Often, these interactions are not planned or prompted, and sometimes they don't involve your teenager leaving their bedroom at all. They are the small moments that happen when your teenager pads into the kitchen to raid the fridge (or to stare blankly into the food cupboard), or when you pop your head around their door to tell them about dinner, or you pass them on the stairs. These are the microbridges across teenage disconnect. They might not sound like much, but when you are trying to build a relationship with someone who is avoiding your company, these tiny, shared moments really matter.

Making the most of these moments requires a light touch. If you are the parent of a teen who has hunkered down in their bedroom, the temptation is to leap on each brief contact to cram in all the parenting you have been storing up for the last 23 hours and 59 minutes. We seize the chance to remind them about their maths homework, check they have tidied their room, complain about a lost permission slip and offload all those pent-up parental transactions that build up because we never get to see them. We resort to a smash-and-grab approach to interaction that drives our criticism-sensitive teen even further into withdrawal. They learn to avoid us even more. The next time they encounter a parent on the stairs, their neurological defences will be primed, and their hackles will rise before you start to speak.

Now, I'm not saying those parental reminders about homework and permission slips never need to happen (though, in chapter 6 I'll explain why they should probably happen a lot less!) but if our priority is to maintain a relationship with our teen, and we have only one momentary shot at it, then using that moment to build rapport might be a smarter choice. Using that moment to remind your teen not about their homework but about your supportive presence and to lay another breadcrumb in the trail for when they need you. It might be just a smile, a "Good morning", a comment about the weather or the dog, some gentle joshing, a compliment – whatever might serve to bridge the divide between you and your unique teen.

Securing time with your teenager isn't always about persuading them to do something, it's also about making the most of those moments when your paths cross, those essential forays into the world that they can't avoid. For many parents, the time we spend ferrying teens around provides our most frequent opportunities to connect. Those moments in the car when, if the mood is right, you might get to chat. That little bit of goodwill that is generated when you help them out with a last-minute lift. Sometimes, building a bridge across the gulf to a disaffected teen doesn't mean luring them out of their bedroom at all. It's the way you pop your head around their door to say good night, the text you send to say well done, the favourite treat you buy them from the supermarket to tempt them into the kitchen. These small gestures and moments can sometimes sneak through at a time when accepting our presence or our love is just too problematic.

If you don't succeed, try again tomorrow

What I'd love to offer you now is a list of brilliant ideas that will definitely 100 percent tempt your teenager out of their bedroom and into your company. And I did try to compile that list, honest. I did the research and I asked an expert – my bedroom-bound teenager. I was hoping he would come up with loads of teen-friendly activities that I could wrap up neatly and give to you. But when I asked my son which ideas were most likely to get him out of his bedroom and interacting with family, he was stumped. Totally blank.

I rephrased the question.

"What could I suggest that is most likely to tempt you to spend time with me or to join in something with the rest of the family?"

"It depends", he said.

I tried again (he's not a wordy chap at the best of times).

"What does it depend on? What's the difference between when I make a suggestion and you join in and when I make a suggestion and you don't?"

At this, his face transformed. We'd found some common ground.

"It depends what mood I'm in", he said. *"It doesn't matter what you say if I'm not in the mood."*

So, there you have it. Timing is everything. Just because your teenager knocks back a suggestion once, doesn't mean it wasn't a good idea or that it isn't worth trying again (and again and again . . .). Some days a banal idea will get a teenager out of their room and happily engaging while on other days, the best idea on earth won't work.

A few ideas from other parents that might help

So, with the above proviso firmly in mind, the list of suggestions below is offered as a starting point. Because, of course, there isn't one perfect idea which is guaranteed to make every teenager happy to hang out with their parents. You know your teenager best – and if it doesn't feel that way right now, then trial and error is a good way forward. In the depths of teenage withdrawal, one of my teens would willingly tag along on a walking trip but under no circumstances would he sit down for a family meal for longer than ten minutes. (We ate a lot fewer meals together than I would have liked but have some wonderful, shared memories of getting drenched in Welsh mountains!)

It might be that your teenager has a passion that will help open their door: fashion, football or saving the planet? Adolescence is a period of intensity and creativity and if you can find a way to share (or piggyback) your teen's passions, fantastic. But if not, the suggestions below (from parents who have been there and done it) should get you thinking. This list comes with a huge caveat, of course. If they're not in the mood, pretty much nothing will get a teenager out of their room – but don't give up, because tomorrow that same idea might work.

Food

Food is great bait for tempting teens into your company. Some teenagers can be enticed by a trip to their favourite fast food or spicy chicken restaurant. I realize that may not be your idea of culinary heaven but the point is spending time with them, not nutritional content, so be prepared to compromise.

PARENT TIP

"Stick to their favourite fast-food brand so they feel like they're on safe territory – but suggest a branch further away where there's no chance of their friends wandering in."

Eating away from home is not just a good way to get teens out of the door, it can help disrupt those repetitive mealtime arguments (over homework and bedrooms, etc) that grind everyone down – and spark some new conversations simply because the environment is different and there are other people to focus on.

PARENT TIP

"Sit so you are both facing the window. They are more likely to chat if you aren't looking at them and it gives you material to keep the conversation going."

At home, buy a sandwich toaster and a smoothie blender (call it a "milkshake maker" if that helps). You are looking for kitchen gadgets that produce easy-to-make teen-friendly snacks that can be prepared rapidly enough to actually get used but which also extend your teenager's grab-and-go raids into the kitchen by a few precious minutes. Anything that encourages teens to linger in the kitchen opens up the potential for moments of connection. Similarly, encouraging them to cook or bake might lure them into the kitchen – where you can strategically wander through and perhaps snatch a few words of conversation!

PARENT TIP

"The arrival of the weekly supermarket shop never failed to get my two into the kitchen and foraging for the good stuff before it was all gone!"

Regular family meals together are a tradition worth fighting for, but it doesn't necessarily have to be dinner. Sunday brunch might be less likely to clash with your teens' other priorities and is a more relaxed opportunity to eat together and make teens feel like young adults. Sitting at a table opposite someone who is asking them questions can be off-putting (even torturous) for a threat-alert teen, so think about less formal seating arrangements. Maybe at a breakfast bar? And, if things are really bleak and there appear to be no routes through to your teen, make use of that smoothie maker yourself, or make a hot chocolate and pop into their room. If their defences are up, you don't even have to say anything, just hand it over and let the whipped cream and marshmallows build a tiny bridge for you.

PARENT TIP

"My daughter and I used to watch *The Great British Bake Off* together and every week we would do a bake. Sometimes, she wasn't up for the baking so I would do it by myself and she would be the judge."

Films/TV

Watching TV together is probably the top tip I hear from parents of teens. Like food, TV provides a focal point which takes the pressure off teens (as they are not the centre of scrutiny). Watching TV demands little from them and lets them engage with you on their own terms. And because they are at home, they have the option to leave whenever they feel like it, keeping the threat levels low, and making it more likely your teenager will relax and drop their guard.

PARENT TIP

"She used to message with her friends on her phone all through the programme, they were all watching it at the same time. But I didn't really mind because she would talk to me too. I'm pretty sure her friends had no idea I was there."

Don't be snobbish, watch whatever interests them (TV is a brilliant way to get an insight into your teenager's current thinking and preoccupations!). Even if there is absolutely no chance their mates will see them sitting with you in your living room, it can help overcome their internalized "imaginary audience" of friends if you watch something their friends would approve of. If your teen is watching *I'm a Celebrity* or *Love Island* or *Married at First Sight*, watch it with them. Reality TV shows that revolve around big personalities and social dynamics tend to work well – the more compelling and conversation-sparking the programme, the better.

PARENT TIP

"One of our favourite shows was *Catfish* – sparks lots of conversations about how people aren't always what they seem and how relationships don't always go the way we think they will. Honestly brilliant. Never would have watched it if it hadn't been for my daughter."

If in doubt, opt for something funny. Just laughing together without talking is still a big win. When we laugh alongside our teens, it activates positive emotions and sends a powerful signal that we are enjoying their company, which is great for their self-esteem and helps hold open a welcoming space for them.

Shopping

Lots of parents go shopping with teenagers as a means of spending time with them. If you're the one with the money, that instantly makes you a desirable companion – and that's a heady temptation for a parent experiencing abject rejection in every other attempt at interaction with a teen. That's also the downside of this route. Shopping involves spending money so it's not an everyday option for most of us. But if it is something you both enjoy, or your teen is happy just to browse, or if there is a special occasion coming up (a prom, a wedding, a birthday), then shopping can be a great way to get time with your teen. Do set a clear budget in advance. Teens can feel a lot of pressure to buy ludicrously expensive designer goods in their pursuit of social status – a pressure they will relentlessly redirect onto the parental wallet.

PARENT TIP

"The thing I like about shopping is not so much the hanging around while he looks through all the rails, it's the getting there. We usually chat in the car about what he wants to buy, which shops we will go to, the brands he likes – I'm not sure if it's just because he is buttering me up but he is chattier than any other time."

Money

Given the enormous pressure teens feel to have all the fashionable kit, earning money can be a powerful motivator for them to engage with the wider world. As we saw in chapter 1, the adolescent brain is especially sensitive to rewards and, for some teens, the prospect of getting paid can help tempt them out of their room. Different parents have different views on whether teens should be paid to do household chores. Personally, my approach has been to have some basic expectations and then attach monetary rewards for the over-and-above tasks like bigger garden maintenance jobs.

PARENT TIP

"I paid my teenager to paint the downstairs of our house with me. He was slow and wasn't good at tidying up after himself but I got a lot of time with him stuck in the same room together!"

Even if they are earning their wages outside the home, driving them to babysit, or to a litter-picking job miles away, is another potential window for conversation.

Get a dog

I appreciate this isn't an option for everyone. Dogs are expensive and require a lot of space and time. However, getting a dog consistently comes out as a top tip from parents of teens. So, if getting a dog isn't an option, have a think about whether you could accommodate an alternative pet. Pets create a central point in a home, a gravitational force pulling teens toward the family which can be a powerful counterbalance to teenage withdrawal. As a focus of joint family love and attention, pets create lots of opportunities for conversations and help bind family members together in a shared endeavour. Pets also provide a safe anchor in a teenage storm; they are there for teens to pour out their emotions to and always listen without judging.

PARENT TIP

"In our house, the first thing my kids did when they got up in the morning or came home from school or came out of their rooms was to say hello to the dog and give him a cuddle."

Of course, dogs have the added advantage that your teen might just occasionally come out for a walk. I'm not suggesting that if you get a dog, your teenager will eagerly skip along with you on daily walks (no matter what kids say when they are angling for a puppy, we all know that the burden of dog walking will fall on their parents). However, a dog is a built-in excuse for inviting teens to come out for a walk. And for every 20 times that you invite them, if only once is successful, that's a win – not least because (as we'll see in chapter 5) walking is a brilliant way to get your teenager to open up to you.

But now, let's turn to the thorny issue of teens and their phones.

CHAPTER 4

THE ANTIDOTE TO PHONES, FRIENDS AND SOCIAL MEDIA

From a parent's perspective, a teen's phone is both a blessing and a curse. Phones empower us to stay in contact with our teens while they take their first independent steps into the world. Phones help parents feel safe and keep us in touch (and if our teen is not responding to messages, there is always that hotly debated tracker function to fall back on . . .). Yet, phones also create a barrier between us and our teen. They get in the way of our relationship.

Smartphones have a magnetic pull for teenagers. It can seem like anything going on in that phone – no matter how trivial – is more important to a teen than interacting with their parent. A message from a friend about what THEY are having for dinner is given precedence over answering a question about dinner that WE have just asked them (or, indeed, eating that dinner with us!). A single lame emoji can outrank us. We try to get their attention, but their eyes are fixed on that little screen. We speak, but all we get in response are huffs and pulled faces (or nothing at all because their ears are stuffed with headphones). If you want to build a relationship with your teenager, getting them out of their bedroom isn't enough. We need to get them off their phones.

The pressure for teens to be on their phones is immense. Digital social lives carry on 24/7 and a teen's drive to feel included [*assimilation*] means never straying too far from their device. Yet those same phones don't always make our teens feel good about themselves. Mean words get messaged, unwisely. Friendships get damaged. Group selfies broadcast to the whole of Teen World who was (and wasn't) invited. And then there is that non-stop flow of tweaked and filtered selfies and ads to compare themselves to (and find themselves wanting).

What we really want for our teens is for them to believe that they are wonderful and valuable and lovable just for who they are. They don't need to look like the people they see on social media or have the gizmos and glamour of mega-influencers. They don't need to cloak their beautiful unique selves with the same branded trappings as every other teenager in order to be likable. We want them to have friends who appreciate them and care about them, and not to feel that their lives depend on answering every message instantly. We want them to put down their phone and do something healthier instead!

And there's the dilemma. Telling a teen not to care what other people think just doesn't work. Telling them not to be so obsessive about their phone won't make any difference (I'm sure you have already tried that!). Worse, it might drive the wedge further between you and your teen and make them less likely to listen to you or to want to spend time with you (after all, you clearly don't understand their lives and what matters to them!). If you want your teenager to come off their phone – for their sake and yours – criticizing them is unlikely to be helpful.

Parents are much more effective in helping teens navigate the perils of phones, friends and social media if we provide a counterbalance to their digital social lives in which our teenager feels loved and accepted exactly the way they are. Teen peer relationships are intense and fraught. We need to make sure their relationship with us is a safe harbour, a place of guaranteed unconditional love and acceptance. That doesn't mean we approve of everything they do, but that our teen feels first and foremost that we are their biggest fan, not their biggest critic. We need to help hold together their self-esteem with our unshakeable positive regard, so they are more resilient to the hurts of modern teen life and less vulnerable to the dangers we fear. And, most of all, we need to walk the walk (not just deliver the talk) on creating a family culture where phones are managed healthily.

Why are teens so obsessed with their phones?

Smartphones are intensely habit forming. Personally, if I'm not careful, I find myself scrolling social media in even the briefest of lulls. Before I know it, the phone is in my hand, the apps are open and I'm rechecking a feed I finished checking only minutes ago. If a message flashes up, or a notification chirps, and I'm unable to read it instantly, I experience a distinct flush of stress. Logically, I know it's probably just another photo from my mother in the family WhatsApp group (carrots she has pulled from the garden or a random collection of redundant objects she is giving to charity) but I feel an urgent need to check that phone, nonetheless.

If adults find this compulsive nature of phones problematic, for teens it is even more of a challenge. Phones are where teens' most important preoccupations all come together – friendship, identity, appearance, fitting in, sex, romance, risk-taking and learning. This is a potent mix for the reward-driven teenage brain. All four of the teenage independence drives – *separation*, *individuation*, *assimilation* and *autonomy* – are activated and facilitated by their smartphones. Phones (plus the apps and cameras in them) are the primary means by which teens communicate with friends, conduct their romances, hone their identity, seek validation and stake their place in their peer group.*

Remember all that brain science in chapter 1? We know that teenagers are primed by their brains to seek social approval from their peers. Feeling left out or humiliated is experienced by teens as a neurological threat – that's not due to lack of perspective, that is actually how it registers in their brain. Teens are neurologically driven to prioritize the opinions and responses of their peers above all others – and those peers live in their phones, laptops and games consoles. Kept away from their digital devices, many teens experience acute FOMO. They quickly become anxious about missing out on an interaction that might be crucial for their social positioning. What if someone says something funny and it goes on to become an in-joke that they are not a part of? Or if a person of influence declares a like/dislike that redefines their friends' views on what is fashionable, and they don't know about it? They might make a mistake, say the wrong thing, or be laughed at – and all because YOU insisted that they put down their phone.

Teens are highly attuned to social hierarchies (who is popular, who is not, who is friends with whom) and they are constantly alert to where they sit in that hierarchy. The sheer speed of the digital world means their online friendship group needs tending frequently. To stay in the loop, they have to check in as often as possible and never break a streak – or the social bubble will just move on without them. Parents of younger teens given phones for the first time are often flabbergasted by the sheer volume of messages exchanged

---

* Not all teens choose phones as their primary device. If your teen is holed up in their bedroom and not attached to their phone, it might be that as you read this chapter, you realize that something similar is going on via a different digital device. Other teens are so concerned about not fitting in that they adopt an "I don't care" attitude and barely use their phones at all, voluntarily excluding themselves from the frenetic online communications that occupy their peers. And, of course, some teens have better balance than others.

every day, even between groups of kids who are spending all day together at school.

Once teens are using social media, this pressure to participate and to perform is even greater. Social media plugs directly into a teen's desire to construct an identity. Through likes and comments, they get direct measurable feedback on how they are perceived, and they can directly compare themselves to others. Even when not looking at social media, some teens will spend hours getting ready for, taking and tweaking photos and crafting clever captions, or planning events which will be deemed photo-worthy, while all the time under acute pressure to hit the send button again in case they drop off the social horizon.

In short, if it feels right now like your teenager's relationship with their phone is more important than anything else in their lives – including being civil to you or speaking to anyone at all at Grandma's birthday party – that's because, to them, it is. Once they jump into the sink-or-swim world of teenage peer group adherence, that phone is their social lifeline.

The impacts of phones and social media

OK, I get it – they care about what their friends think. But it can't be healthy to be on their phones ALL the time? Most parents feel instinctively that phones are somehow not good for teens. We have real worries about how this eyes-down, phone checking, selfie-taking lifestyle is affecting their physical health, their mental health, their body image, their literacy, their life skills, their communication skills, their social skills – and, indeed, every other aspect of their health and development. Surely, living via the medium of screens cannot be good for them?

When we read the news and speak to our friends, these worries seem completely justified. Parents see teens whose lives look completely different from our own at that age, devoid of so many of the healthier hobbies that we value and that our children used to love. We see daily media stories about the harms teens are exposed to online, and we fear the pernicious effects of all that screen time on their young brains. More and more teenagers are seeking support for mental and emotional health issues, a tidal wave of mental health struggles that coincides exactly with the rise of smartphones and the encroachment of handheld digital devices into childhood. Without question, these two facts must be related?

However, the picture emerging from research is not so clear. Evidence on the links between screen time/social media/phone use and adolescent wellbeing is inconsistent. This is partly because there are so many different studies looking at slightly different things, for slightly different age groups and measured in slightly different ways. Good quality research takes time and the pace of change in our personal use of technology is outstripping the research. Experts are reluctant to make concrete recommendations without robust evidence, so they tend to sit on the fence. For example, the US surgeon general has cautioned that at present it is not possible to determine whether social media is safe for children and teens.[*] In the meantime, parents are left freaking out at headlines comparing smartphones to crack cocaine and worried sick at news of yet another tragic death due to exposure to harmful content online.

So, what do we know for sure? Most research studies do seem to show that there is an association between excessive screen time and poorer mental health for young people. However, there is no consensus on what counts as "excessive" or where the cut-off point for safe use might be. This negative link between high levels of screen time and teenagers' wellbeing is relatively small when averaged out (smaller than the link between teen wellbeing and poor sleep,

---

[*]   May 2023.

as an example) but these averages mask important variations for individuals. Different teens seem to be impacted by tech use in different ways at different times in their adolescence. It is not clear what the key features are of those teens who are most likely to be impacted negatively by tech, but it seems likely that teens who are more vulnerable offline are more vulnerable online, too.

It is also important to note that this is a correlational rather than a causational link. That means we don't know whether excessive screen time causes poorer mental health or whether teens who already have poorer mental health tend to spend more time on screens (or, indeed, if the impacts are bi-directional with each factor increasing the other).

There do seem to be some upsides to teen technology use, too. For example, there is fairly consistent evidence showing that teenagers who have extremely low levels of internet use (or zero time online) are also more likely to have poorer mental health. This is probably because the digital world is such an important source of social connectedness for modern teenagers and social isolation impacts teens acutely.

When it comes to social media and self-esteem, the picture is similarly mixed. Since teens are so sensitive to feedback from their peers, it's not surprising that some teens report that social media impacts on how they feel about themselves. But not all teens report this impact and, where it occurs, it is not always a large or a negative impact. Indeed, a small minority of teens report that their self-esteem actually increases when they use social media. At a time when talking to their parents may not be easy, many teenagers say they derive support and a sense of community from the internet and that it helps them find people with whom they have similarities or experiences in common. This is especially true where teens don't have access within their real-world community to people who share important aspects of their identity. Young people crave a sense of belonging and many teens report finding positive affirmations of their sexuality, gender identity, race or disability (or just their hobbies and preoccupations) in their online worlds.

But what about those teenagers who are negatively influenced by what they see online? Being able to find your tribe at the click of a button can be affirming. But it is not such a positive factor when the tribe you find is, for example, dangerous or unhealthy, one that valorizes self-harm, unhealthy eating, extreme thinness or misogynistic aggression. The problem with social media is that it tends to serve us up more of what we linger on, and there is no guarantee that your teenager will not linger for a moment on something dark or harmful.

Rather than presenting teens with a wide range of viewpoints and lifestyles, the algorithms that drive the content of our social media feeds tend to narrow down our digital worlds and pigeonhole us – which can have the effect of amplifying idle curiosity into a daily stream. If it is football gossip, cute puppy videos or adverts for shoes that we are being streamed, that might get annoying but it's probably not harmful. However, if an already vulnerable teenager with body image anxiety starts being served repeated posts about extreme dieting and they start to find their sense of acceptance and belonging in that tribe, that's dangerous.

So, although parents are justified in being fearful about the dangers of the internet and about the numbers of teens who are struggling with their mental health, pinning all the blame on phones or social media isn't supported by evidence. Those digital devices are neither definitely safe nor definitely dangerous. It depends on what your teen is looking at, and on their unique vulnerabilities.

Where does that leave parents? Well, we are right to be concerned and to be alert. But if we want to limit the potential negative impacts of phones and social media, then constantly having a go at our teen for being on their phone is probably not going to help. As with everything to do with parenting teenagers, relationship is key here. A better way to help teens navigate these challenges is through a strategy of warmth and acceptance that builds their self-esteem and opens up communication, and by creating a whole-family culture in which wellbeing is prioritized and there are plenty of healthy buffers around tech use.

But before we dive into what that might look like in practice, now might be a good time to cast your mind back and remember what it felt like to be a teenager. This is one of my stories (I am sure you have your own).

PERSONAL STORY

THE PARTY I WASN'T INVITED TO

I was 13 years old and my best friend (who lived next door) had dumped me. I was a year younger than her, and she'd fallen in with a much cooler crowd. I was desperate to be accepted by them.

On the night of her 15th birthday party, I put on my tightest pencil skirt and walked back and forth past her house for over an hour. In my mind's eye, I figured those cool guests would see me in my grown-up skirt and want to hang out with me. What actually happened was that I got the rough end of some bitchy comments from a gaggle of arriving girls.

I went home, raided my dad's drinks' cabinet and cried myself to sleep. The next day, I got up, shrugged it off as best I could and pretended it had never happened.

When I look back at that night, I can see how silly I was. I shouldn't have cared so much. I shouldn't have tried so hard. I shouldn't have allowed those stupid comments to hurt me.

But I can still feel the hurt. Those teen emotions were real. It mattered to me deeply – which is probably why I remember it so vividly even now.

Fortunately, I am almost certainly the only one who does remember my humiliation that night. We didn't have smartphones when I was a teenager. I can only imagine how much worse it would have been if those snarky comments had been written for everyone to see on a group chat. Or if someone had taken a photo of me and circulated it on social media.

Nor did I have to scroll through a stream of group shots of everyone having an amazing time doing the one thing in the whole world I had wanted to do – but from which I had been so pointedly excluded.

How can we help teens feel good about themselves?

I'm pretty sure that an adult telling me not to care that I hadn't been invited to that 15th birthday party wouldn't have made a jot of difference. Trying to counter a teen's FOMO by telling them not to care what other people think, is pointless. They do care. They don't really have a choice; their brains are programmed that way. If adults want to protect teens from the potential negative impacts of phones, friends and social media, one of the most important things we can do is to support their self-esteem – and that is unlikely to be achieved by telling them they are getting life wrong.

Good self-esteem is one of the best buffers a teen can have against a multitude of vulnerabilities. Self-esteem is the internal opinion we hold of our own abilities and worth. It is our overall sense of the type of person we are and of our value. Self-esteem is not an objective fact, rather it's a subjective conclusion we draw from our interpretation of our experiences. Self-esteem doesn't always accurately reflect how good or bad we are at anything, just how we feel about ourselves.

A person's self-esteem is influenced by three key factors: feeling *accepted*, feeling *competent* and feeling *effective.*

- Feeling *accepted* is about knowing you are loved and valued and belong exactly the way you are.
- Feeling *competent* is about feeling capable, that you are able to rise to challenges and have strengths and talents (in some areas at least).
- Feeling *effective* means believing that what you do makes a difference, that you have some agency or control or impact.

It is the feeling *accepted* part of self-esteem that explains why children so often experience a dip in their self-esteem when they move into the teenage years. The teen years are all about testing how *acceptable* you are [*assimilation*] and that inevitably brings with it a whole heap of self-doubt and insecurity.

So, what helps? When teens are feeling insecure about their peer relationships, they need more than ever to feel secure that their parents are on their side. That we believe they are lovable and worthwhile. That we value them. Teens care deeply what parents think about them (even if it doesn't always seem like it). If we belittle their priorities or dismiss their preoccupations, or don't take their concerns or hurts seriously, they not only withdraw further from us, they take our poor opinion of them with them and blend it into their own.

If we are to hold on to a relationship with our teens and build their self-esteem, we need to make sure our relationship with them is a safe space, a place of guaranteed unconditional love and acceptance, and that our teens know this. We want them to feel utterly secure in the knowledge that they are special to us and loved by us – that they are significant, valued and enjoyed. It's not enough to think it, you have to show it. And you need to be genuine in this. If you are saying positive things to your teen out loud while internally rehearsing the learning point you want to make next (or the ways in which you want them to change), it won't work. You need to remind yourself as often as possible how much you do love your teenager (despite the hurtful things they do). Hold them in your mind's eye as the truly wonderful and amazing young person they are – albeit a wonderful and amazing young person who is struggling with the pressure and demands of a difficult transition and, perhaps, not always being nice. It stinks being a teenager. It hurts. If we could short-circuit the learning they need to go through, we would. But we can't. The one thing we can do is to be on their side. To be the person in whose eyes they see themselves reflected as truly lovable and *accepted*.

I know that's hard to do when they are giving so little back (and maybe getting so much wrong). But we are far more likely to influence how our teen feels about themselves and bolster their resilience through a strategy of radical acceptance rather than criticism or correction.* When they raise their gaze from their phone, we want them to see warmth and kindness in our regard, a reminder that no matter what is going on in that stressful online dance of social acceptance, we love them exactly for who they are. They might think we're goofy or soppy and bat away our love, but they will see it. You might feel like you are failing because you aren't "teaching" them anything, but this positive regard and radical acceptance is a powerful antidote to those harmful impacts you fear from their phones and social media.

---

* Dr Gordon Neufeld and Gabor Maté sum this up brilliantly in their book *Hold On to Your Kids*: "We have to give to kids what they cannot give to one another: the freedom to be themselves in the context of loving acceptance – an acceptance that immature peers are unable to offer but one that we adults can and must provide." Dr Gordon Neufeld and Gabor Maté, *Hold On to Your Kids: Why Parents Need to Matter More Than Peers* (Vermilion, 2019), page 126.

When teens feel loved and accepted by us, they are far more resilient to self-doubt, and to the ups and downs of the struggle to fit in.

When teens feel secure that there is no scenario in which we won't love them, they are far more likely to come and tell us if there is something troubling going on.

That doesn't mean that we just leave our teens to navigate their phones, friends and social media all by themselves. But a light touch is needed. We need to start from a point of acceptance. Stand in their shoes – if it matters to them, it matters. By accepting how important it is to them that they stay in touch with their friends, you build trust. Whereas spend too much time suggesting better ways for them to go about things, and they will soon start to feel like you're the enemy rather than a supportive team member.

Make it as easy as possible for your teen to talk to you by lowering the stakes. Take your good opinion of them off the table – that is not in jeopardy. They have it, no matter what. Signal to them your profound belief in them and their ability to rise to a challenge even when they've lost their way.

> *I know how much your friends matter to you, that's understandable. Wanting to be a good friend is a wonderful quality. I think your friends will see how wonderful you are and still want to be your friend even if you miss this one event.*

If we engage positively with our teens about their phone life, if we accept their concerns and invite their ideas and opinions in a way that signals our positive regard and belief in them, we not only make it more likely that they will talk to us about what they are doing on their phones, we build a connection which makes it more likely that they will put down that phone and engage with us. By showing them that we believe they are *acceptable*, *competent* and *effective*, they are more likely to believe it too, and will be less vulnerable to the negative impacts we fear for them.

ACTION POINT

Research has shown that five positive interactions are required for every negative interaction in order to sustain a good relationship.

A positive interaction might be a smile, a gesture, a hug, a comment, a kind word.

Do a quick audit. Think about today, or yesterday, or this week (or look at the messages between you and your teen as a prompt).

How many positive interactions can you remember? How many negative? What was the ratio? What could *you* have done to tip the balance more toward positive interactions?

A blueprint for pushing back on phone time

So, you're saying we should just stop nagging them and let them have their phones 24/7? Far from it. Experts may not be able to say for certain what screens are doing to teens' brains, but we do know that tech use is habit forming. Left unchecked, it quickly expands to fill increasing amounts of time, displacing other more positive activities. Building a teen's self-esteem will help protect them from many online harms (and hopefully predispose them to engaging in real-world activities), but parents also need to be alert to excessive tech use getting in the way of those lifestyle factors we know definitely are good for teens – for example, exercise and sleep. When teens are choosing doom-scrolling and cat videos over positive healthy pursuits, that is a problem.

A modern teen's world is extremely noisy when they have a smartphone. When I was a teen (and probably you too), we could retreat to our bedrooms and get some respite. Bedrooms were a space to dress up, to daydream, to read, to write, to draw, to listen to music, or just sleep. Teenagers today take all their friends (and enemies) into their bedrooms with them in their phone. If there is no sanctuary for teens to take a break from their devices, that's a relentless pressure. Parents need to find ways to protect space for non-tech activities in teens' lives. We need to help them learn to manage their mind health actively and create some breathing spaces from the incessant demands of a digital life.

At last, you've got to the bit I wanted to hear all along. How do I get my teenager off their phone? I'm not sure you are going to like the answer! When it comes to phones, a whole-family approach works best (I'll talk specifically about gaming in chapter 6). That means that you are going to have to change your habits too.

A whole-family approach means fostering a family culture in which looking after one's body and mind is valued, in which there are rituals for regularly coming together tech-free and a set of whole-family habits which create buffers around the encroachment of phones into everyone's lives. Here's the plan:

Aim for balance

There are so many things that are potentially detrimental for teen wellbeing – lack of sleep, lack of exercise, poor diet, skipping breakfast – if your teenager has disengaged from you and is barely coming out of their bedroom, then trying to tackle all these issues at once would be disastrous. Put aside any doom mongering or should/shouldn't thoughts and aim for a bit more balance rather than total perfection.

When it comes to phones, that means sidelining them rather than banishing them. If bringing their phone along means your teen is going to spend time with you or engage in a healthy physical activity, that's still a win. If there is a part of the activity where you really don't want them to be on their phone, negotiate and clarify that in advance (and remember to compromise).

Even better, use those collaborative planning skills from the previous chapter to engage your teen in absorbing activities where phones are naturally sidelined. You know your teenager best and what will appeal to them (and if it you're not sure where to start, experiment and keep trying). For one of my teens, high adrenaline ideas worked best for tempting him off his phone – theme parks, kayaking, abseiling – anything with a hint of danger. (I went down A LOT of zip wires with my heart in my mouth and my eyes squeezed shut while being laughed at by that particular teenager.) If your teen is a bit of a gamer, activities with high thrill/risk factor (such as paintballing) or strategy skills (such as boardgames or escape rooms) might appeal. For other teens, smaller doses of more creative activities will succeed in keeping their phone in their pocket (maybe try cooking or crafting?). Remember, the teenage brain is reward-driven, so seek out low-tech activities your teen enjoys and do them as often as possible. And that phone will naturally stay out of use just a little bit longer.

Be a good role model

Tech is a whole-family issue. As parents we need to model to our children how to regulate our own phone use and look after our mental and physical wellbeing. Teens are the first to call hypocrite on adults who complain about them using their phones while we are so frequently on our own devices. If you are scrolling social media in bed last thing at night, why shouldn't they?

If you want a teenager to put down their phone, you need to switch off your own devices too. If your teen never sees you reading a book or exercising or having a conversation without a phone on the table right in front of you, you can't expect them to do those things either. We need to model to our teens positive mental health habits, and make sure they see us incorporating good physical health habits into our daily lives. And we need to find opportunities to talk with them (not to lecture, to discuss!) the benefits of different habits and the importance of creating space for a quiet mind. We need to put our values where are mouths are and show them that tech-free time matters enough for us to do it too, and how we can all take small steps to look after ourselves.

We also need to model a healthy relationship with the tech that we do use. Turning the TV off when no one is watching it, and curating our own social media feeds so we only follow accounts that help us feel connected and good about ourselves (rather than those that make us feel ashamed or like we are failing in some way).

Designate tech-free spaces

A healthy family life needs some designated tech-free spaces. These might be physical tech-free zones in your home – like no screens in bedrooms (which I highly recommend) or no screens at the table when you are eating (which I also highly recommend!). Or you might have tech-free times – like no screens in the mornings, or after 9pm, or maybe tech-free Sunday afternoons – whatever fits with your family's home and routine. These no-tech times and places can't just apply to teens, they must apply to everyone in the family (adults and visitors included), with no exceptions.

Talk with your teen about why tech-free time is important. This isn't about criticizing our teens, it's about us all taking responsibility for caring for ourselves and each other.

I know your phone is really important to you and I don't want to stand in the way of you communicating with your friends. But I also think it's important for all of us to have breaks from our phones too. Can we have a think together about how we can create regular opportunities for us all to give our minds a bit of a break?

Designated tech-free buffers could take the form of low-tech family rituals and traditions – such as eating regular meals together, Friday night board games, Sunday afternoon walks, or Saturday morning sports (spectating or playing). The more we can use routines, rituals and habits to create low-tech spaces, the more we can avoid getting into oppositional dynamics over every bit of tech time. So, keep eating together and playing together as long as you possibly can.

Being able to tolerate boredom tech-free and come up with ideas for things to do is an essential part of a balanced childhood. For teens, especially, the constant dance of social approval (both in the real world and online) is stressful. Creating no-tech buffers within family life provides sanctuary spaces for everyone to rest and reset, and find some calm.

Put distance between people and phones

Where is your phone right now? Most likely, it is within arm's reach. And when phones are within reach, the research shows that we do reach for them. We reach for them when we are watching TV. We reach for them during conversations. We reach for them first thing in the morning and last thing at night. The most effective way to regulate phone use is to put phones out of reach.

When you are at home, put your phone in another room so you are not tempted to check it every few minutes. Or have a designated shelf or drawer where all the phones live. If you want to use your phone, go to it rather than always taking it with you. When you are out and about, carry a book to read so you don't have to reach for your phone to fill bored moments.

Make nighttime a non-negotiable phone-free space. Set a time in the evening when phones are put away (yours included). If a teen has their phone in their room, no matter what they say or how adamant they are that they won't look at it, they will use it. The research is utterly consistent on that. If they say they need their phone for music to fall asleep to or as an alarm to wake them up, buy them an alarm clock and an audio player that can't access the internet. Sleep really matters, especially for teens. Keep games consoles out of bedrooms too (or make them easy to remove each night). Poor-quality interrupted or insufficient sleep impacts learning, mood and mental health. This is one of those matters over which you should stand firm in the face of teen opposition for as long as humanly possible.

Take as many opportunities as you can to separate yourself and your teen physically from your phones. If it's in their room or in their pocket, it will get used.* On family holidays or day trips, think about putting all the phones in a safe place (or in a single bag) and agreeing specific windows when everyone can have some phone catch-up time. With younger teens, delay giving them a smartphone as long as you can (don't rush to be the first). Start with small doses of phone time and strict rules and only move the boundaries slowly.

Press reset if it has all gone awry

I'm not suggesting you will be popular with your teen by trying to set some boundaries around everybody's devices. You won't. Phones really matter to teens, and they are likely

---

* Ben Brooks, in his highly illuminating description of life as a modern adolescent, compares asking teens to resist their phone when it is on their person to "suggesting they walk around with a pocket full of marshmallows and only take a small nibble of a single piece once a day". Ben Brooks, *Every Parent Should Read This Book: Eleven Lessons for Raising a 21st-Century Teenager* (Quercus Books, 2021), page 31.

to push hard for what they want. When it comes to tech, most parents are just doing the best we can and making it up as we go along. We don't always get it right. Lots of us get badgered into allowing teens to have phones in their bedrooms and, despite our best intentions, end up drifting into a situation where individual handheld devices are filling everybody's downtime.

It's never too late to make a change. With preteens and younger teens, you might opt for a top-down parent-led reset if tech time has gone too far. But an alternative would be to use this as an opportunity to practise some collaborative problem-solving (and I'd definitely recommend that approach with older teens). If you present this as a whole-family issue (rather than a teen-specific problem) which requires jointly agreed solutions, any changes you make are more likely to stick. Sit together down as a family. Talk about your concerns, outline some ideas and invite everyone else's ideas. The changes you end up with this way might be smaller than you wished, but those small gains and incremental wins are still important. And there will have been a bit more goodwill generated (or at least, not so much lost!) in the process.

That goodwill is essential. Ultimately, smartphones are not inherently good or bad, it depends how we use them. Your teen might be using their phone for friendships, emotional support, researching hobbies or just for entertainment. They could be feeding their self-worth or their self-loathing. They could be being bullied, buying drugs, viewing disturbing content, or just doom-scrolling to avoid difficult thoughts and feelings. Our aim as parents of teens isn't just to tick a box on a that imaginary Good Parenting Scorecard by limiting their phone time, it's to have a relationship with them in which they feel able to disclose these issues to us and to seek our help. We can't control teen tech use in a way that eliminates all risk, but we can aim for a relationship in which they feel safe to talk to us. And that will mean learning to listen (and maybe finding out things that are hard to hear).

A QUICK RECAP

WHAT HAVE WE LEARNED SO FAR?

- The teenage drive toward independence has four key elements: *separation* (from parents), *individuation* (defining their identity), *assimilation* (fitting in), *autonomy* (making their own decisions).
- The teenage brain goes through a unique developmental phase that supports these four independence drives. The middle part of their brain (which governs emotions, rewards and threats) easily overwhelms their more reasonable thinking front brain.
- Separation can be hard on parents. Whatever you are feeling is OK, but getting stuck in unhelpful thinking patterns can lead to conflict or withdrawal dynamics.
- Five Golden Rules: be kind to yourself; manage your thoughts (to manage your feelings); model the behaviour you want to see; handover the power; prioritize relationship over principle.
- If you want your teenager to spend more time with you, use collaborative planning and make the most of small moments to connect.
- Phones (and other communication devices) matter to teens because they activate all four independence drives.
- Bolstering self-esteem and a whole-family approach for screen time are likely to be more impactful than criticism or authoritarianism (especially for older teens).

CHAPTER 5

HOW DO I GET MY TEENAGER TO OPEN UP?

Being positive in our interactions, making allowances, managing our own feelings and being collaborative to maximize even tiny bits of time together – these will all go a long way to building trust and tempting your teenager out of their bedroom more often. But when those fleeting moments of connection are over and teens retreat back into their rooms, parents are still left with the fear: that pervasive nagging anxiety that so many parents of teens carry inside us that there might be something going on, something we're missing, something they're hiding, something we need to worry about.

Teenagers can be fiercely protective of their thoughts and feelings. Some teens will bat away parents' concerns angrily, while others just close up and retreat into monosyllabic answers. We know our teens are vulnerable (and the news is full of the horrors that could befall them) but when they shut themselves away, how can we know if this is just normal teenage behaviour or if there is something more serious going on? How can we find out what they are thinking and feeling if they won't talk to us?

The temptation is to go hunting for clues. Indeed, many parents resort to searching teens' bedrooms or raking through their messages or social media activity to find out what's going on in their lives. And there may be times when that is the right thing to do (such as when you have a strong suspicion there's something dangerous going on). But even if you discover something via that route, you will still need to talk to your teen about it. And you'll need to find a way to engage them in a discussion that leads to understanding and positive change – or you risk them just carrying on regardless but getting better at hiding things from you.

When we are worried about our teens, it can feel like what we are searching for is information and certainty, but what we really need is insight. Take cannabis as an example. If you discover concrete proof that your teenager has been smoking weed and you jump into a lecture on all the reasons why drugs are bad for them, the chances of you having a positive impact are minimal. Because you haven't stopped to understand why they've been smoking weed. Maybe, they were pressurized by their friendship group into a situation they didn't feel they could get out of? Maybe they are feeling socially isolated, so they wanted to look cool? Or maybe they're smoking weed to numb their thoughts and feelings because they are finding life tough? If your goal is to support your teen's wellbeing and influence their choices positively, then knowing the answer to that question is important.

To have those types of conversations, the ones that truly help you understand what's going on for your teen so that you can respond in ways that will help, you'll need to learn to listen and pause before you talk. Being the trusted adult that a teenager opens up to is all about demonstrating again and again that you won't overreact, that you won't judge them and that you will respect their thoughts and feelings (and not think badly of them) no matter what they disclose.

Why teens close up

The developmental drive to separate isn't just about teens separating physically from their parents. A key part of the independence project is teens taking ownership of their own minds. While younger children might reveal their inner worlds spontaneously in chat and play, teens are usually much more circumspect about what they divulge.

There can be many reasons for this secrecy. Your teen's desire for privacy might simply be part and parcel of their drive to carve out a separate psychological space [*separation*]. By keeping their thoughts to themselves, they are claiming governance of their own headspace and asserting their right to choose who they grant entry to [*autonomy*]. Oftentimes, this guarding of their headspace is fuelled by self-protection. Exploring one's thoughts, sexual desires and identity is much easier to do if you can carve out a private space where there is no danger of being seen or feeling judged – and, especially, of being judged by a parent who has a habit of believing they know you better than you know yourself. By closing up mentally – or by emitting aggressive Keep Out signals – teens create a barricaded space from where they can reveal new bits of themselves in small, curated snippets, so their whole self (and their whole self-esteem) is never placed under threat.

Sometimes, teens put up a wall of silence to safeguard parental love. When teens become secretive, it's more than possible that they have something to hide, something they don't want parents to know. They might be doing (or thinking about) something we wouldn't approve of, like vaping, drinking or sexting. Parents often assume that teens hide these wrongdoings to avoid parental consequences but often it is fear of losing our good opinion that weighs most heavily in their decision-making. Contrary to what they might say, your good opinion really does matter to your teenager. Teens don't want to upset or disappoint us.

We are the foundation underpinning how they feel about themselves and when we think badly of them it confirms their worst fears that they are unlikable or failing. So, when there is difficult stuff going on, teens will often try to deal with it themselves, or resort to lying and cover up, to avoid losing our positive regard.

However, the biggest reason teens don't open up to parents is due to fear of how we will react. When researchers ask children (of all ages) why they didn't talk to their parents about something difficult going on in their lives, the most common response is that they were worried their parents would overreact. That we would get upset or angry or take control of the situation and do things they didn't want us to do.

And, let's be honest, they're not wrong in that fear, are they? If your teen does let on that there is something wrong, you will probably want to do something about it, won't you? To give them advice or intervene in some way. But that's not what our teens want. When children open up about a problem, it is seldom because they want the other person to fix that problem. It's usually so they can understand the problem better by articulating it and to find some relief through sharing. Teens don't always understand exactly what's going on inside them. Talking is a way of exploring their thoughts and shifting some of their stuck feelings.

It's the same for adults. When we are alone in our heads, we are often a jumble of thoughts and feelings. When someone we trust asks us "How are you feeling?" and we attempt to put that inner jumble into words, that's when we start to understand what's actually going on. And for that to happen, we need to be given a little space to amble and linger in our disclosure, and not fear that we will be cut off by the person on the other side of the conversation jumping in and telling us what we should be doing or how we should or shouldn't be feeling.

ACTION POINT

Think about the people you feel comfortable talking to about your most vulnerable issues. What do they get right? How do you know it is safe to talk to them?

Compare this to someone you've learned not to open up to about difficult topics. How do they make you feel? Do they make you feel judged? Dismiss your concerns? Give advice? Get impatient? Or just don't get it? What do they say and do that makes you feel that way?

Which category do you think your teenager would put you in?

What teens hear when parents talk

When teens won't open up to their parents, there is a pretty good chance it's because they've decided we are rubbish listeners who jump to conclusions, prioritize our own agenda and make them feel rushed, judged and misunderstood. To be fair, that's not entirely our fault. The teenage brain is primed to detect attack so, even if parents are incredibly careful, teens are liable to take our well-intentioned messages the wrong way. We might think we are making a helpful suggestion but, as far as the ever-vigilant teenage amygdala is concerned, our offer of advice is an existential threat.

What teens hear when parents make suggestions

Teens are driven toward independence. And independence means doing things by yourself without help from others. So, when parents offer help, an independence-seeking teen hears a threat. They hear criticism. They hear us saying that we don't think they are grown-up enough to get it right. They don't hear our good intentions; they hear us treating them like a child. Remember, the teenage brain is especially sensitive to social threats. Anything that makes them feel disrespected or humiliated or low status is going to set off their neurological alarms and initiate a defensive response.

What teens hear when parents offer help

Even simple offers of support can land as an attack on teenage autonomy – especially when these offers come from parents. We are the people they need to separate from to achieve independence, so their amygdala has even more reasons to be jumpy when they are talking with us. (Which is why your lovingly meant advice might be thrown back at you, while exactly the same words from a grandparent or mentor will be accepted as wisdom and taken on board!) Unless carefully delivered, teens are just as likely to feel attacked as comforted by our messages of support.

So, how am I supposed to get through to them? I'm walking on eggshells here! Communicating successfully with teenagers can mean treading a delicate path, that's true. Ultimately, like every aspect of parenting teens, it comes down to building a two-way relationship. If your agenda is to "get through to" your teenager, or to give them advice, or to gift them your hard-earned wisdom in order to short-circuit their own learning, your communications are likely to fail. But if you can learn to hold back your suggestions, listen with acceptance and true curiosity, and provide a non-threatening space for them to explore their thoughts and feelings, then you'll be the parent your teenager wants to talk to.

How to be the safe person a teen wants to talk to

To create a safe supportive space for a teenager to talk, you'll need to keep things calm and avoid triggering their threat response. The best way to do this is by practising empathetic listening. Empathetic listening isn't something that always comes easily to parents. Even when we are great listeners for our friends, we can struggle to get it right with our own children. We feel responsible for our children, like it's our job to make sure their lives go well (whereas with our friends, we are more comfortable just being a sounding board). When our children tell us about their problems, our instinct is to jump into Fix It listening (which isn't really listening at all).

We rush to fix the problem by giving advice and telling them what they should do. We try to fix their difficult emotions by reassuring them that it will all be okay, and listing all the reasons why this problem that feels so huge to them isn't really such a big problem at all.

What teens hear when parents reassure

Empathetic listening is the opposite of Fix It listening. Empathetic listening is not about changing your teen's mind or making them feel better or giving your opinion. It is simply about making your teen feel heard. Signalling to them that you hear what they are saying, and that you recognize how they are feeling. Acknowledging what they are experiencing without passing comment or telling them how they should be feeling or what they should do. Listening without judgement, from a place of acceptance. *This is where you are, I see you. I see you are hurt. I see you are angry. I see you feel scared that you won't be able to do it. I see you feel hate for yourself. I see how much this matters to you. I see how hard this is for you.*

Empathetic listening means not assuming the role of expert or advisor (your teen is the expert in what they are feeling and thinking right now). It means listening with a view to increasing understanding (yours and your teen's) rather than listening for the purpose of formulating an answer. Get it right and your teen might just give you a glimpse of what the world looks like and feels like to them.

If that all sounds hard or unfamiliar, follow this five-step plan to get you started.

STEP 1: Pay attention
If your teen is expressing an emotion or telling you about a problem, stop, listen and pay full attention. Tune out the alarm bells from your own worry radar and just focus on listening calmly to what they are saying and how they are saying it. If your teen is emotional but isn't talking (and it feels like the right moment), you could take a tentative guess to open up a conversation.

I don't have a window into your mind to see what's going on inside you so I might be wrong, but from the outside it looks like you are feeling a bit low. Is that how it feels on the inside too?

STEP 2: Summarize
Don't pass any judgement on what your teen says. If they tell you they hate their body, don't contradict them and tell them their body is wonderful or that looks don't matter, just accept that is how they feel right now. When there is a pause, summarize what you have heard and name the emotion you think they are experiencing.

It sounds like you really don't like how you look at the moment.

It sounds like you're pretty angry you didn't get the grade you wanted on that test.

That seems really unfair you haven't been invited. No wonder you're feeling hurt.

Summarizing what they've said and naming their emotion not only signals that you are listening, it is also therapeutic.

It helps teens get a handle on what's going on inside them. And, if you have got it wrong, they will correct you.

I absolutely hate my body. I don't want to be in it. I'm so ugly.

STEP 3: Keep calm
Control your reaction. Create a calm atmosphere by keeping your voice low (in volume and pitch) and speaking slowly. Breathe. This will help you to stay calm by activating your parasympathetic nervous system and also signals to your teen that you are not panicking or about to fly off the handle. Our teens need to know that we can cope calmly with whatever they bring to us, no matter how big or bad it feels for them. And if they see us staying calm and coping with their big feeling, that goes a long way toward reassuring them that this hard feeling is something they can cope with too.

If what your teen is saying is alarming or triggering for you, try to catch your own shock and keep it contained softly inside for you to process later. We are aiming to be empathetic (to show that we see and understand what they are feeling) rather than empathic (joining in and matching what they are feeling). Try to keep your facial expression soft and kind – teens have poor facial recognition skills which means they are more likely to misread people's faces and detect negative emotions or intentions when there are none.

STEP 4: Explore gently
Allow your teen lots of space, control and choices in difficult conversations. Don't rush to fill gaps in the talking, allow silences and pauses. It might take a bit of time for your teen to find words or feel brave enough to speak. If the conversation stalls, just reflect back to them again what you have heard and be gently curious.

I hear you. You hate your body. I can see how hard that feels. Do you want to tell me a little more about how that impacts you?

You might need to return to this conversation and revisit it over a period of time as trust grows.

STEP 5: Problem-solve together

Rather than rushing to offer your solutions, ask your teenager what they want to happen next and how you can best support them. Avoid giving advice, and especially avoid the words "should" and "shouldn't" (these are judgements masquerading as advice). Instead, draw on their expertise and resources.

Have you found anything so far that seems to help?

What ideas have you had that might be helpful?

Agree next steps (even if that's just that your teenager is going to think about something) and undertake to talk about it again.

Thanks for talking to me about this, I really appreciate it. It helps me a lot to understand what's going on for you. Have a think about what you want to do and let's talk about this again tomorrow.

If you can learn to listen in this supportive way, not only will it have a therapeutic impact on your teenager and help them learn to understand and manage their own emotions, but it will also build a relationship in which your teen feels confident to open up to you again.

You can use empathetic listening for big issues and small, for when teens are upset by the actions of a friend or for when they disclose deeper uncertainties about who they are or how they feel. You won't get it right every time, and that's OK. Empathetic listening takes practice. If you get it wrong and lose your cool or jump in with suggestions, go back and revisit that conversation. Apologize and hold your hands up that you got it wrong and allowed your emotions to hijack your brain. You might explain that you love them very much and sometimes that makes you panic when you are worried about them. Then ask for a second chance so you can try again.

A PARENT ASKS ABOUT SELF-HARM

"My daughter is self-harming and I don't know how to help. She refuses to see a professional. I can't understand why she's doing it. Is this something she has copied from friends? I'm a single dad and no clue what it's like to be a teenage girl."

I'm so sorry to hear that your daughter is struggling. If you have no experience with self-harm, it can be baffling to work out why someone would deliberately hurt themselves. And, of course, when it is our child who is being hurt, that can trigger some deep and instinctive responses in us.

Right now, I don't know why your daughter is self-harming, and nor do you. The first step is to have a calm, open and non-judgemental conversation with her. Not a conversation that is trying to fix the situation – a learning conversation in which you try to understand what is motivating her self-harm.

Be honest. Explain that this is not something you have experience in, that you've never been a teenage girl and that you don't know what it's like to be her. But that you want to try and understand. You can see she is struggling with some really big feelings.

Keep your voice low and slow. Leave lots of spaces for her in the conversation (it might take her time to find words and courage) – this will also give you a chance to breathe and regulate your own build-up of emotion.

Once you have created a sense of safety and calm, you could ask some gentle questions around whether there are specific thoughts or feelings or situations that tend to trigger her self-harming? Does it tend to happen at a particular time? How is she feeling just before she self-harms? How does she feel afterwards?

There are many reasons that people self-harm. Often, it is a coping strategy that brings temporary relief to overwhelmingly difficult feelings or intrusive thoughts.

If you are going to help your daughter, it's important to understand when your daughter is self-harming (the trigger) and also what she is getting from the self-harm (the effect). I know that might sound odd, but self-harm tends to be cyclical. Difficult thoughts/feelings build up to a crisis moment that is alleviated in some way through self-harm. However, the relief is only temporary, so these unmanageable thoughts/feelings then build up again, and the self-harm is repeated in the next crisis moment.

Signal clearly that you are listening carefully by repeating back to your daughter what she says (without judgement or comment). *"So, the feelings build up until it feels like the only way to stop them is to bruise yourself. Have I understood that right? And then you feel calmer?"* I know you want her to stop the self-harming but try not to rush to fix things and be mindful to manage your own anxiety (breathe!).

By talking calmly and curiously with your daughter, you may be able to help her identify and understand this cycle – which is the first step toward breaking it.

You might not get far in a single conversation but, however far you get, remember to thank your daughter for her trust and reassure her that you're there for her (and ensure injuries are treated appropriately). Remember, the calmer, safer and less judged she feels talking to you, the more likely she is to turn to you in crisis.

Once you have built some trust and understanding, you'll be in a much better position to work with your daughter to find other ways to manage her thoughts and feelings and to explore what professional support she might need to do that.

(For further advice on when to seek help and where to go, see chapter 9.)

Small changes that help good conversations happen

Good conversations are built on a foundation of trust and connection. We can't just go marching into our teenager's bedroom and demand they open up to us. If you have taken to heart the previous chapters, you'll already be on the lookout for how you can maximize micro-connections with your teen through small everyday moments. For the big conversations to happen, we need to build regular bridges across the divide of teenage withdrawal.

Big conversations happen much more easily when there are smaller incidental conversations for them to grow from. Even trivial conversations can provide useful building blocks for constructing a relationship in which teens feel safe to talk. I vividly remember a time when texting a photo of our dog to my son was the only guaranteed way to ensure he responded to my messages. So, I sent A LOT of pictures of the dog. These microbridges can help fan even the tiniest flame of connection. The next time you see each other, you can talk about that photo, where it was taken, and maybe a family memory of the dog. It's a little message of warmth and love that builds the goodwill from which other conversations might grow.

These are delicate flames to fan but if you want to create positive opportunities for conversations to flourish, there are some small but important adjustments you might want to make when communicating with your teen.

Choose your moment

By which, of course, I mean choose *their* moment. If there is an online conversation going on with their friends (or even just a silly cat video on TikTok to watch), then that is probably going to take priority over talking to you. If your teen is feeling churned up about something that has happened that day, this won't be a great time to talk about future careers or college choices. And it's hard to shoehorn a great conversation into a brief meeting on the stairs.

Communicating with teenagers involves patience – being in their company, doing things *they* enjoy, talking about meaningless stuff until the right moment presents itself for a few moments of real communication to take place. It is a worthwhile investment: those little nuggets of communication are the threads that hold your relationship together.

Sometimes teens will come to you when it's the right moment for *them* to talk. Often, that will be the wrong moment for you, such as late at night when you are desperate for sleep or when you are rushing to get out of the door. Your teen will appear in the room and something big that's been on their mind will start tumbling out, or you'll hear the quiet words "Can I talk to you for a minute?" Or they'll just plonk themselves in front of you with an air of openness or expectancy and start to chat. If you possibly can, seize those moments and go along with them (even if you are longing for your bed!). Take every conversational bridge that's offered.

Try side-by-side

Conversations when you are side-by-side (such as in the car, walking the dog or sitting on the sofa) or when you are busy doing something together (watching sport or cooking a meal) often flow more easily with teens than talking face-to-face. If you have something difficult you need to talk about, try going for a walk together or for a chat in the car. (Don't jump on every car journey as an opportunity to bring up big issues, though. Some teens can feel a bit trapped in the car and will clam up or get angry if you try and talk to them there. If that's your teen, try to find activity that gives them an easy escape route where they can opt in or out of a conversation. They might feel less pressured and more likely to chat.)

When you are both busy doing something else, your teen is likely to feel less scrutinized. Body language is more likely to be relaxed. Pauses and silences will arise naturally and be more comfortable, creating a bit of space in the conversation. With other things going on, there is less pressure and conversation often flows a bit more easily. You might just be talking about football, but flowing conversation (no matter what the topic) is a good habit to cultivate.

Don't talk about them

Direct questions often put teenagers on their guard or make them suspicious that you are trying to prise something out of them (their secret thoughts, or a confession about what they have done wrong). That will bring their shutters straight down. An indirect approach often works best.

Chat about their favourite characters on a TV programme. Talk about yourself, the neighbours, family members, or celebrities. Sometimes teens will engage enthusiastically in conversations about other people when they won't talk about themselves – and in a way that gives you a wonderful insight into their opinions and thought processes. Use natural launchpads for these conversations: something in the news, a bit of gossip you have picked up about their school, something you've seen on social media. Be indirect and their hyperalert amygdala won't even realize you are being curious about them!

If you want to talk about effort and reward, start a conversation about sport. If you want to talk about gender or body image, talk about pop stars. If you want to talk about prejudice or changing social norms, talk about grandparents. These indirect conversations are much more likely to get your teenager expressing an opinion and (incidentally) revealing their thoughts. And if you don't like the thoughts they reveal, remember to engage with them rather than just dismissing their views. If your teen starts spouting misogynistic rhetoric or arguing about trans rights, don't hurry to contradict them, pick up the topic and explore it with them.

That's a controversial viewpoint. What's led you to that conclusion?

Even if you are uncomfortable with the subject or disagree with your teen's take on it, these are the issues they are interested in and through which we can learn about them and meet them where they are. So, run with any conversation that's offered. (The phrase "*Some people would argue that . . . .*" is especially helpful when you want to posit an opposing viewpoint without turning a conversation into a confrontation!)

Ask, don't teach

No one wants to talk to a bore. Don't jump on every conversation to draw out a lesson or say the same things again and again. I know you have valid points to make, and you are concerned to make sure your teen hears them. But conversations need to be two-way. Cultivate conversations where you are not the expert. That might mean being curious about your teen's world or asking for their help or expertise. For example, if you are worried about sexual imagery they might encounter online, there is a good chance they already know a lot about the issue. So, don't barge in with your opinion, be curious about what they already know and what they can teach you.

> I read this article the other day that said the average age a boy first sees porn online is 11 years old. I was really surprised by that. Does that seem right to you? Do you think kids in your school started watching it that young?

Be conversational, don't preach.

> That really worries me because lots of porn is really violent. Do you think young people feel pressure to copy what they see in porn?

Use respectful language

Remember that old adage, "Speak how you would be spoken to"? You need to walk the walk and talk the talk when it comes to communicating with teenagers. Model the style of communication you'd like your teenager to adopt. If you don't listen, or if you use sarcasm or shout or belittle others, then you must expect that to come straight back at you. Speak to them like the responsible young adult you want them to become.

Ask before you give advice.

> Are you just offloading, or would you like me to give my ideas?

If you are giving advice, label it clearly as your opinion and couch it in empowering language that demonstrates you believe they are mature enough to look at things from different perspectives. For example, you might say:

> *These are the things I would take into consideration, but you might have other things that are important too.*

> *I've learnt that this works for me, I don't know if that's something that might work for you?*

> *On balance, my advice would be . . . (but it is your decision).*

Respectfully delivered, soft touch advice often lands well (even if your teen rejects it at the time).

If you genuinely don't think they are mature enough to manage new freedoms sensibly, you still need to find a respectful way of communicating this. Try locating the problem in you, not them. Rather than saying,

> *I don't think you're old enough to go to the shopping mall for a whole day with your friends by yourself.*

A more respectful way of couching this might be,

> *I know you are growing up fast and I am struggling to keep up with that. I'm not quite ready for you to spend a whole day out with your friends but maybe if we could agree a shorter time, or somewhere closer to home, then that might help me in realising that you're ready for that level of responsibility.*

Of course, there might still be an almighty row about it, but you will have at least maximized your chances of future discussions by taking a respectful approach. . .

USEFUL PHRASES (FOR BYPASSING THE THREAT-ALERT TEENAGE AMYGDALA)

When you want to say this	→ *Say this instead*
What's the problem?	→ I get the feeling you might have something on your mind at the moment?
We can fix this problem.	→ I see your problem, that's a hard one. I'm here if you want support or to work through it together.
Here's what I am going to do to sort this out for you.	→ Is there anything I can do that would help?
This is what you need to do to fix this problem.	→ Have you got any ideas that might help? What have you tried so far?
I think you should do X.	→ It's your decision. If it were me, I would probably think about doing X.
These are all the reasons why you should definitely do X.	→ It's your decision. But these are some factors you might want to consider . . . I'll leave you to think about it.
I think that's a really bad idea.	→ I wonder what might happen if you do that?
I totally disagree with you.	→ Some people would argue that . . .
What are you going to do about it?	→ Have a think about it and we can talk again later to go through ideas.
I can't believe you did that.	→ That was a big call. How do you feel about it?

Let it go, don't push through

If a conversation becomes fraught, don't keep going or try to push through. Once a teen's emotions are in the driving seat, you are unlikely to have a rational conversation (that part of their brain just isn't firing). If you persist in trying to make your point in these moments, you will just end up feeling frustrated at not being listened to, and unwise things might get said that do real damage.

When your teen is holed up in their bedroom much of the time, it's tempting to rush at a conversation whenever we spot an opportunity and try to land our message no matter what. For example, if you're worried about your daughter's eating habits, or her relationship with food, that's a conversation you need to make happen. And, yes, when she's in the kitchen preparing a snack might feel like a good moment. But if your thoughtfully prepared opening gambit generates an angry reaction, you are better off letting it drop and revisiting the issue another time when she's calm.

If you persist with conversations when things are heated, there is a risk you'll end up making the next conversation go exactly the same way. The emotional regions of the brain that are activated when teens respond defensively are also the region where the teenage brain lays down memories. So, a situation that has previously been stressful or emotional or negative for a teenager is likely to re-trigger those same emotions again and again every time it happens – until even just the thought of talking to you (or the sight of you appearing at their bedroom door) induces an instant negative reaction. They will start assuming you're going to say something that you weren't and will launch into defence mode before you even open your mouth. Or just avoid being in the kitchen at the same time as you.

If a conversation is not going well, just let it drop and move on. Once their rational brain is back online, you'll be able to have that conversation another way. Make the bulk of your conversations good ones, and your teen is a lot less likely to avoid talking to you and much more likely to tolerate your company (at least a little more often!).

CHAPTER 6
BUT ALL THEY CARE ABOUT IS GAMING!

That's all well and good, I hear you say, but having a positive conversation when your teenager is manically jiggling a controller and won't take their eyes off the screen is not so easy. When teens withdraw to their bedrooms, gaming can be a big part of the picture. Not only does gaming lure them into their rooms and make them less likely to venture out, but it can also become a big bone of contention between parents and teens when teens prioritize yet another game above doing their homework or helping out around the house (or, indeed, above doing anything else at all!).

An obsession with gaming often comes hand in hand with other teen habits parents find hard to swallow, such as apathy about schoolwork, monosyllabic communication (or downright rudeness) and a tendency to sulk or do the bare minimum when forced into any non-gaming activity. This is not a state of affairs that fosters good parent–child relationships. Being treated like a servant by an ungrateful teenage lodger who hoards cutlery and can't be bothered to change their pants seldom brings out the best parent in any of us!

Teenage gamers don't just retreat into their bedrooms, they retreat into an alternative reality, a parentless eddy in the teenage space-time continuum. This makes the challenge of staying positive and building a good relationship with them even greater. We want to reach out and connect (and we want to galvanize them into action!) but more often than not we just end up nagging. Or getting sucked into a cycle of conflict and alienation which starts with gentle nudges, progresses to draconian threats and ends with us giving up the fight and throwing up our hands in despair because nothing seems to work.

Telling a teenage gamer to "Turn off that game!" every few minutes is both exhausting and ineffective, and it does nothing to make your teen want to spend time with you. So, what can parents do to connect with a gaming teen, encourage healthier habits and shepherd them into responsible adulthood?

Why do teens love their consoles?

Gaming holds a special lure for teens because it offers an opportunity to exercise all four of their independence drives at the same time. A gaming console is your teen's portal to an entirely separate world where you have no place and no power [*separation*]. In game world, teens can assume different identities and switch between characters at the push of a button [*individuation*]. These gaming avatars often have swagger or command respect [*assimilation*]. In the real world, your teen might be sat in their bedroom surrounded by discarded socks, unfinished schoolwork and empty crisp packets, but as a gamer they are building cities, completing complex missions and making split-second decisions [*autonomy*]. When they take off that headset, they risk feeling like an awkward teenager, whereas in game world, they can feel skilful and heroic. Games allow teens to feel so much more significant, more accomplished, more *adult*.

This alternative universe is where many teens find their tribe and their social status. Eavesdrop on a teen's conversations over their headset and their speech (and vocabulary!) is totally different; they don't sound like themselves. That gaming console is your teenager's equivalent of a preschool dressing-up box – it allows them to enter an imaginary world and be someone else.

The problem is that gaming is much harder to walk away from than a dressing-up box. Gaming plugs straight into the pumped-up reward-driven limbic regions of the developing teenage brain. When we have a pleasurable tech experience, it releases dopamine in the brain, a reward chemical that makes us want to repeat the experience. Games are purposely designed to keep hitting our reward buttons often (for example, through points systems, badges, medals and levels) while always holding out the prospect of an even bigger reward you can unlock if you keep on playing.

The teenage brain gets an especially big neural kick from rewards. The back-to-front progress of their brain development means the reward centre in their brain is running on superfast 5G while the thinking front part of their brain is still on intermittent 3G. This makes teens much more prone to hitting that Play Again button and less likely to pay attention to any warning thoughts about negative consequences (such as an assignment left unfinished or an angry parent). Future-based thoughts about consequences are housed in the weaker front part of their brain and are easily drowned out by the immediate technicolour thrill of another game.

To adults, prioritizing gaming over schoolwork (or over showering or spending time with family) looks like misplaced priorities and poor judgement but, neurologically, it's much harder for your teenager to follow through on their good intentions. Teens don't make the decision to keep on gaming in a mature and considered way. The good judgement part of their brain lacks neurological fire power to take control when their "I want MORE" reward impulses are all revved up. As a result, it is perfectly possible for your teenager to care deeply about their school performance and sincerely intend to hand in their best assignment ever, but still end up gaming late into the night.

Neurodivergent teens are especially prone to developing a gaming habit as they often have even less neural weaponry for resisting temptation and controlling their impulses. Similarly, if teens are smoking cannabis or drinking alcohol while gaming, then their chances of self-control are diminished (in which case, see chapter 9 for advice). When teens are gaming with other teenagers, that's an additional factor that makes gaming difficult to stop. Even when they want to moderate their behaviour and turn off the game, the threat of losing social status by being the first one to bail out is a powerful deterrent. Teens are far more likely to make risky or reward-driven decisions when in the company of their peers (which is why car insurance companies offer lower premiums for teens who don't give lifts to their friends!).

It might not look like your teen is being overly adventurous just sitting in their sweatpants eating snacks, but for some teens, the risk-taking element of gaming can be a big part of the pull.* Many online games involve an element of jeopardy – such as leaping across platforms, avoiding projectiles or losing a life. For some teens, this online risk-taking functions as a bravado shield against much scarier real-world risks, a make-believe gaming bubble which insulates them from the fear and stress that come crashing in when they engage with the real world. The teenage years are a time when academic and social pressures significantly ramp up, and this can be overwhelming for some teens. When this pressure to step up

---

* As a side note, I'm not aware of any research studies to back this up but quite a few parents of gamers have told me that the activities most successful in getting their teenagers out of their bedrooms were the high-adrenalin ones that replicated the high-thrill factor of gaming – such as theme park rides, mountain biking, bouldering or anything that involved trying not to crash and getting slowly more skilled with practice (eg skateboarding, surfing, rafting, etc). That might be worth some thought if you are struggling to engage your game-loving teen in any other activities.

a gear is greater than a teen's belief in their ability to succeed, some teens will opt out and choose not to try – not to try at school, not to try socially, not to try at young adult life. If they don't try, they can't fail. Withdrawing into gaming is the perfect way to avoid difficult real-world challenges, but still protect a sense of self-worth by becoming expert in a craft their peer group admires.

From where you're standing, this obsession with gaming, and your teen's failure to step up and take responsibility for real life demands, probably looks like laziness, or not caring, or just not understanding how important it is to do well at school and get a good job. It probably feels like your teen simply can't be bothered to do their homework and would rather fritter their time away on a pointless game. However, on the inside, there might well be a young person who understands perfectly how important this all is but who is paralysed by the scale of the task and struggling to believe in themselves. When teens say they don't care – about school, about the future, or about what you think – there's a good chance that what they really mean is they care a lot about those things, but the weight of those expectations feels too great. Far easier to avoid the whole thing (or put in grudging, minimal effort) and let your brain tune out those intrusive thoughts with a pleasurable gaming experience.

Being the parent of a gamer

So, what am I supposed to do? My teen does zilch. They have no motivation, no get up and go. Trying to get them to switch off their game and do their homework is like pulling teeth every single day. They are driving me nuts. Understandably so. A teenager's compulsion toward gaming might be explicable but it is intensely frustrating for parents, especially when it gets in the way of healthy habits, family time and pretty much everything else we value. And it is hardly conducive for building a good parent–teen relationship. Trying to motivate a gamer to direct their energy toward other more important activities can feel like pushing a boulder uphill. Or, perhaps, like baiting a tiger. Because gaming doesn't bring out the best in our teens. Late-night gaming disrupts sleep, making teens harder to rouse in the mornings, more prone to emotional outbursts and less able to concentrate on schoolwork. And teens are much quicker to anger when their emotional brain is in ascendance. Interrupting a game to tell a teen to get off their device can provoke a nasty and aggressive backlash.

However, the biggest complaint I hear from parents is the total waste of time, talent and potential that gaming represents. Parents are told at every stage of parenting that it is our job to support our children to fulfil their potential. That we are responsible for our children's success. Most of us are willing to accept that our children can't be the best at everything – but we still want them to be the best version of themselves. And we believe it's our job to help them become that. So, when we see our teen wasting their time and talents, or not doing as well as they could do, or not even trying, we panic. Because that means we aren't doing our job well, we aren't good parents. Those thinking traps come crashing in and we start catastrophizing like crazy.

Time is running out. They are screwing up their lives. If I don't get them back on track right now, they will fail their exams and end up bedroom-dwelling dropouts who never hold down a job.

Naturally, we try to galvanize our teens into action. We start off being gentle and reasonable. We explain to them how important it is to do well in their exams. When that doesn't seem to make an impression, we remind them. And then we remind them again. Reminding turns into lecturing, but with no effect. Our language turns increasingly critical in our desperation to get through to them. Maybe we start labelling them lazy and irresponsible (we know we shouldn't, but we are just so frustrated). Then, before we know it, we are marching into their rooms to rip that console plug from its socket – which is not at all helpful for relationship building.

It's at this point that many parents (battle weary and teary) throw in the towel and decide to just leave their teens to it. We decide there's nothing more we can do so we get off their backs to avoid the conflict and preserve whatever is left of our relationship. *It's their life. They are going to have to figure it out for themselves.* We try looking on the bright side. *It could be worse. At least I know where they are and they're not getting into trouble.*

Maybe we feel grateful that they are safe in their bedroom, and not out on the streets falling prey to gangs or crime or bullying. But then we remember, these risks are on the internet too, and we start to fret. An article pops up in our news feed which says video games makes teens more prone to addictions. We hear something on the radio about loot boxes* being a gateway to gambling. We catch a glimpse of another teen's accomplishments on social media and start to panic that our teen has already fallen too far behind and we spin back into a cycle of recriminations and conflict.

> *Turn off that stupid game and get your act together. Life is not a game. You need to start putting in the effort because life is serious and if you don't do some work, you are not going to pass your exams and you are not going to get into college. Are you listening to me?*

It doesn't work, of course. Not because they aren't listening – actually, they are registering everything we say. When we label our teens as lazy or irresponsible (out of desperation,

---

* Many online games reward players with loot boxes containing random rewards with the chance that these might include rare or highly prized rewards (though most do not). The most sought-after rewards can be traded within the game, and sometimes bought and sold for money.

fear or frustration), they hear that loud and clear. They hear that they are failing to meet our expectations, that they are disappointing us, and that weighs heavily on them. But it doesn't lead to action.

Why do parents feel it's so important to push teens to "fulfil their potential"? What does that even mean? You probably feel like this is a positive stance. *It's just about supporting our children to be happy and believing in them, isn't it?* Telling our gaming teens how smart they are and how much potential they have (if only they'd put down that console) might be our way of trying to build them up but, codedly, what we are really saying is that they should do better, that they are currently not doing well enough, that they are failing to meet our benchmarks. There might be some truth in this but by focusing on the gap between their "potential" and where they are right now, we risk making our teens feel ashamed rather than motivated.

Teens need us to believe in them here and now, no matter what, not in some future or idealized version of them who gets life right. Potential isn't even a real thing, it's an imaginary construct, the person WE think they should become. It's a maybe-under-certain-circumstances. We all have potentials we don't fulfil. Maybe I had the potential to become a decent tennis player, who knows? I never kept at it long enough to find out.

The pressure to fulfil potential

Frankly, who your teenager could be if circumstances were different is irrelevant. The teenager in front of you is the person you need to work with.

But I don't want them to make life harder for themselves. If they'd just get off that console and do some studying or get a job or just LEAVE THE HOUSE, then at least they would be moving forward. Parents often believe that when our teens aren't stepping up to the challenges of life, that this is our problem to solve. But really, this is your teen's problem to solve. Teens need to figure out their own motivations and learn to manage their own behaviour in order to transition into successful young adults. We can help, but we can't do this for them. In fact, when we take on the challenge of motivating an unmotivated teen, we often actually get in the way of them learning to take responsibility for their own choices and motivating themselves.

Rather than focusing on your teen's behaviour (the gaming), it might be more helpful to think about the why (what's driving your teen's gaming?). Sometimes, when teens withdraw into a games console, they are using it as a crutch because life feels too difficult. Maybe your teen's gaming is a coping strategy for low mood or anxiety, a way of numbing difficult thoughts or feelings or avoiding situations that unsettle them? In which case they are unlikely to make progress until they move forward on those deeper issues (we'll talk lots more about mental health in the next two chapters). Or perhaps your teen lacks the self-confidence to put themselves out there and go for other goals? Or they just haven't developed the self-control to turn off the console? Whatever the reason behind your teen's gaming, our deeper job right now is to support them to develop the emotional skills, motivation and self-belief to move themselves forward. Because no potential is getting fulfilled around here until those start to grow.

When I speak to parents of young adults who had seemed completely lost in their teenage years (to gaming, to weed, or to an undesirable set of friends) and I ask them what changed, what made the difference and how they helped their teen find a better path, the common thread in their answers is always that their teen found something they wanted to do, something that they cared about, a passion, a motivation, a reason to act. And usually, this passion was nothing like what their parents expected for them. We used to call teens who were slow to mature "late bloomers". I find that such a helpful image. Unfortunately, in our hypercompetitive school systems, they are often now labelled underachievers. Try not to get sucked in by this. Some teens take a little longer to grow into themselves, and that's OK.

In the meantime, while we are waiting for them to blossom, the best way we can help our young gamers is to support them to develop some self-regulation and try to stop gaming taking over their lives completely so that they can find the path they want to follow.

PERSONAL STORY

CONVERSATION WITH MY 21-YEAR-OLD (AN ERSTWHILE DEDICATED TEENAGE GAMER)

Me: Do you do much gaming these days?

Him: No, not really. Occasionally. When I'm round at a mate's house, as a social thing.

Me: What changed, do you think? Why do you do less gaming now?

Him: I don't know really.

Me: Did you lose interest? Did your mates stop doing it? Do you have less time? Or do you just have other things you prefer doing instead?

Him: A bit of all of those, I think.

Me: So, in the book I'm writing, I want to give advice to parents on what to do if their teenager is gaming all the time. Is there anything parents can do that would be helpful? Or that they absolutely shouldn't do?

Him: Hmm, just try and get them out of their room, really. You know, encourage them to do other things.

Me: And if they don't want to?

Him: Just keep trying, they'll come out eventually.

Me: What about the ones that never come out? I think that's what parents are scared of, that they'll end up with a 30-year-old living in their bedroom still gaming all the time.

Him: [*laughs*] That's probably not going to happen. They'll get bored in the end. Or hungry. Or they'll get a girlfriend or start going to the pub and get a job. That's not a sensible thing to worry about.

Why nagging doesn't help

So, how do we nudge teens toward self-regulation and self-motivation? What works? Well, let's start with what doesn't work: nagging. The problem with nagging is that it doesn't hold your teen accountable in any way, and it leaves the problem firmly in your hands not theirs. It lets your teen off the hook. Nagging positions parents as the powerholders and sets up that oppositional dynamic that is so unhelpful when it comes to parenting teenagers.

Right now, if you are doing a lot of nagging, the truth is that you are taking responsibility for your teenager's choices. You are the one who is caring how long they are gaming and telling them to switch it off (effectively allowing them to outsource their self-control responsibilities). You are the one who is worrying that they don't do anything else and trying to motivate them toward other activities (so they don't have to motivate themselves). You are the one fretting about their schoolwork and insisting that they do it (effectively backing them into a corner where the only way for them to express their independence is not to do their studying). Nagging means you are working harder on your teen's behalf than they are, and probably feeling intensely annoyed and unappreciated for your efforts. And if you are working harder to secure your teen's success than they are, there is no opportunity for them to develop the motivation, self-control and self-belief needed to make their own future happen. By maintaining control through nagging, we create a dynamic in which lying in bed (rather than doing their homework) makes your teen feel like an independent decision-maker – even though in our eyes it looks like an utter abdication of responsibility.

Nagging also sends the signal to our teens that we don't believe in them, that we think they aren't capable of handling a situation or taking responsibility. By stepping in to take the reins, we signal *I don't think you can do this, you need me to do it for you*. On the flipside, by stepping back and handing over control, we send the signal: *You've got this. I believe in you.* If we want our teens to leave the cocoon of their bedrooms and go find some drive and self-belief, that will require them to do something difficult. Teens are far more likely to rise to a challenge if they are feeling good about themselves and experiencing a bit of success rather than constantly being criticized for their failures.

The fact is you can't nag a teen into motivating themselves or believing in themselves. For that, you have to hand over the power and "parent forward". That means holding teens accountable for their own choices and letting them learn from the consequences of those choices. These consequences might be:

- *positive consequences* (such as praise or feeling proud of themselves);

- *natural consequences* (such as a school detention for being late, or a favourite T-shirt that can't be worn because they haven't washed it); or
- *structured consequences* that we put in place to help nudge them in the right direction.

Rather than nagging them about what they haven't done, it is far more effective to let consequences do the heavy lifting for us and focus our words on building their self-belief by calling out their progress and successes.

Well done for getting to school this morning, I could see you were tired.

A bit of positive recognition is not only more motivating, but it also holds open the door to connection in a way that criticism and nagging does not.

But if I don't nag him to do it, he won't do it at all! This is a bit of a chicken-and-egg situation (which is why so many parents find it difficult to do!). The developmental stage of a teenager's brain makes it harder for them to think in advance about consequences. But experiencing consequences influences their brain development and makes them more able to take heed of potential consequences. When we jump in to rescue teens from every negative outcome (by prompting or reminding or nagging them to do things), they don't experience that vital learning cycle.

ACTION POINTS

Do an audit of your nagging.

- Take a look on your phone at the thread of messages between you and your teen. How many of your messages are reminders, prompts or nagging? (You can spot these by looking for phrases like "Don't forget . . ." or "Please can you . . ."). How many of your messages contain positive comments about things your teenager has got right?

- Keep a diary for a week. (Do this on your phone using voice notes to make it super easy). Make a note every time you prompt or remind your teen to do something. Look back over all those reminders. What were the consequences for your teen when they didn't do the thing you asked?

Setting gaming limits for younger teens

Giving up nagging doesn't mean we just abandon teens to their consoles. This is about making teens accountable and handing over responsibility in bite-sized chunks. If you are stuck in daily battles with a younger teen over obsessive gaming, now is a great time to put in place a system in which their choices have consequences. Of course, you don't want them on their console all day and night, so you'll have to structure the choices available. I'm not talking about using threats (*Turn it off or I will do something you don't like!*) – threats tend to escalate conflict with teens rather than defusing it. This is about genuinely giving teens the power to choose either way (*Choose A and X will happen or choose B and Y will happen,*) but weighting the consequences in order to lead our teen in a positive direction.

One of the easiest ways to do this with a younger teen or preteen is to position gaming as conditional on certain other choices being made first. For example, if you are concerned that your teen's gaming habit means they have no balance or they aren't doing any other positive activities, then you might structure their choices by making gaming time contingent on participating in sports or non-tech hobbies first. If your concern is that they aren't doing anything to help out around the house, then completing their chores could be the precondition for gaming time. What we want is for gaming to come about as a consequence of other positive choices rather than as something that gets in the way.

Isn't that just treating them like a kid? I think it's treating them like an adult-in-the-making. We're not telling them what to do, but we are making them accountable for their decisions (which is at the core of being a responsible adult). If they decide not to do their chores, they don't get gaming time. Rather than us holding the reins and trying to yank them along the right path, we're handing over the reins. But we are structuring the paths available (so they can't choose to game 16 hours a day) and making one path more attractive than another.

You can make this system even more adult by formalizing it into a written contract (signed by you both), stipulating how much gaming time is acceptable and the conditions under which gaming is allowed. If it helps to gain some cooperation from your teen, start off by agreeing an allowance of how much time they can have playing games each day (on a console or computer) with no strings attached. Be sure to make this time allocation smaller than your teen will want but also smaller than the maximum gaming time you are prepared to allow. If your teen wants additional gaming time on top of their allowance, that will be dependent on other conditions being met first – and these can be laid out clearly in the contract. For example, your teen could earn additional gaming time through participation in positive extracurricular activities, so 90 minutes of sports club after school earns an extra 30 minutes of gaming, or completing all their chores by 8pm on Friday might unlock extra hours of gaming time at the weekend, or handing in all homework due that week might result in more time allowed for gaming on Saturday. Structure the choices to encourage the positive changes you want to see in your specific teen's life. Of course, they can still choose not to do their chores or their homework. However, if you weight the contract smartly, and stick to it consistently, there's a good chance they will be motivated to follow it.

Exactly how much choice and control you hand over depends on your teen's age and maturity (and how entrenched their gaming habit might be). With younger teens, you will probably want to be quite directive and specify limits on when their extra gaming time can be used (for example, at the weekends only). With older teens, you might give them more freedom to choose when they game. But if they blow their whole weekly gaming budget on a Friday-night binge, there is no more gaming until the clock resets on Monday. (That's a great way to encourage self-regulation, but you must be prepared to weather the storm and stick to your guns if they get it wrong!)

The first time you attempt a gaming contract, lots of things will go wrong. You'll discover an unforeseen loophole or perverse incentive that you hadn't anticipated. The gaming time they end up with will either be too high or too low. You'll realize that you have no way of checking whether certain conditions have been fulfilled. Your teen will shout at you for the choices they have made. But persist. Review the contract after a week to tweak it and then keep reviewing it fortnightly or monthly to adjust the terms according to changing circumstances.

I'm not claiming you are going to be popular by doing this. And it involves a lot of parental effort and consistency. But if you can do it calmly, with warmth, respect and collaboration, hopefully you'll find a way through. Rewards are much more powerful incentives for teens than threats of negative consequences. And remember to keep pointing forward to the future.

> I understand that you don't like this system, but if you can work with me and show me that you can make good choices and stick to an agreement, then I'll be able to see that you are responsible, and we can talk about shifting some of those rules.

What we are trying to do is to foster accountability. So, the more collaborative you can be in negotiating the contract the better.

The earlier you can implement this type of rule-setting with teenage gamers the better. I'd suggest as soon as there is a console in the house or, at least, as soon as it becomes clear that your teen or preteen is prone to its pull. Using a gaming contract doesn't mean you don't put any other tech boundaries in place. Those whole-family tech-free buffers we talked about for phones (in chapter 4) should also apply to gaming gadgets. Keep gaming consoles out of bedrooms for as long as possible, or be prepared to disconnect and remove them when time is up.* Set non-negotiable rules around nighttime switch off times (and don't budge on them).

What if I've left it too late? There's no way my teen would agree to any of this and, anyway, I'm not around to supervise whether they're sticking to it or not. If you feel like the ship has sailed on rule-setting, and you have an older teenager, then you might want to take a slightly different tack and instead channel your Jedi parenting skills into guiding them toward healthier choices and a more positive routine.

---

* Advice from personal experience: don't rely on just removing their controller at night – even the most disorganized teen gamer will find a way to get hold of and hide a second backup controller to get that dopamine hit!

Persuading a dedicated gamer to change routine

Daily routines are really important because they help to embed our habits. These can be negative habits like staying up until 3am gaming, or positive ones like getting up in the morning, completing homework, exercising regularly and helping out around the house. When you are in a routine, choices become more automatic. Getting teenagers into a positive routine therefore helps them to develop self-discipline around essential tasks and can help reduce repeated conflict around contentious issues.

I'm not suggesting that encouraging an unmotivated teenager into a good routine is easy. You are going to have to manage your frustration, employ all those smart conversational strategies we looked at in the last chapter, and summon up warmth, belief and positive regard (at a time when these are probably in short supply) in order to tread a narrow collaborative path between your own principles and your teen's current inclinations. This is Jedi parenting indeed. But by approaching change this way, you will be treating your teenager like the responsible adult you want them to become and modelling the relationship you want to be in.

Arrange a time to sit down together and discuss it.

I seem to be nagging you a lot at the moment about schoolwork*/gaming*/chores* [*delete as appropriate] which isn't much fun for either of us. I'd like ten minutes to sit down and come up with a plan together so we can stop arguing. When would be a good time today or tomorrow for us to do that?

Give them input on when (not if) the conversation happens. By planting the seed and positioning them as mature participants in the issue, you might (just might!) avoid them feeling ambushed or dictated to. If they try to avoid the planned conversation, softly, firmly insist. Try to pick your moment wisely but do make that conversation happen.

Start off by asking them for their thoughts rather than by launching straight in with a complaint or solution. Even if they don't think there is a need for change, explain calmly why it is causing you a problem.

> *I care about you and it's important to me to support you in making good decisions around your schoolwork and your wellbeing. At the moment, I'm getting frustrated because things don't get done when I am expecting them to happen so I end up nagging you and we end up arguing. It would be really helpful to have a clear plan that we both agree on when you are going to do your studying, so I can back off and leave you to it.*

Don't react to any missiles they throw into the conversation. Treat every comment as a contribution. You need to stand down your own reactive amygdala here and breathe!

> *My idea is you just back off and let me get on with my life my way!*

> *Yes, that probably would be easier for you in the short term. But I care about you and I don't think that would be the responsible thing for me to do as a parent, and I don't think it would be great for you in the long term, so we are going to have to come up with compromise ideas.*

Don't expect your teen to have the same priorities as you. Instead, deploy your empathetic listening skills. You are not aiming to convince them to see the world your way. The goal here is to work with them to agree a marginally better daily routine.

> *But I don't care about school.*

No. I can see that schoolwork isn't lighting your fire right now and you're not motivated by it. But school is a fact of life so let's see how we can make things work a bit better for you.

Ideally, we want to harness our teen's goals. If they are hoping to go to college (despite making no effort toward it), then try to identify one small change they could incorporate into their routine that would take them one step closer to that goal. If, on the other hand, they have absolutely no motivation to do anything other than gaming, accept that feeling. But don't accept how it is being manifested.

I get it. Right now, you don't care about the future, and you don't know what you want to do when you finish school. That's OK. You're a teenager and you have plenty of time to figure that out. Maybe in a year's time, you'll suddenly decide you want to become a chocolatier. Maybe in five years' time, you'll discover a love of engineering or computer programming or mountaineering. I don't know. You don't know. In the meantime, let's keep you healthy and well and make sure you keep as many doors open as possible until you figure out which one you want to go through.

Invite them to come up with ideas. You might think that the best way to approach studying is to get up at 6am on a Saturday morning and get it all done before breakfast but there is no point insisting that your teenager follows that schedule if they are dead set against it. You know what will happen – they will just ignore the 6am alarm and put it on snooze for three hours. Instead, talk to them about when they study best. What works for them? What are the fixed points in their day? Is there a particular time when it is most important to them to be gaming (for example, because that's the time when most of their mates are online).

Identify what needs to be done and when and where the gaps are in their day. Discuss how many hours of gaming are reasonable on a school day. You might find it helpful to use a visual schedule where you block out the fixed points and you can both see clearly which pockets of time are available (this also gives you both something to look at which can bring down tension levels).

Work collaboratively with them to scope out a possible routine. Try to identify in advance potential blockers and enablers. Gaming is habit forming, and change is difficult, so you might need to factor in some rewards to help them stick to their routine. For example, a Friday night gaming binge as a reward for making a change that week. Identify some positive enablers by asking *What would help you stick to the routine?* They might need some practical support (such as a whiteboard in their room or a new alarm clock). Or you might be able to support with small treats to support their motivation – their favourite pizza if they come through and do all their chores that week.

The routine you come up with doesn't need to be perfect – even small incremental wins are worthwhile. You are not going to end up with your ideal routine. You may not even think their ideas will work. But agree to try their best ideas for a week and see how it goes – with the proviso that you'll come back together to review it and, if it isn't working, try out some different ideas instead. Set an early review period. Then, if the routine isn't working or falls apart, you can tweak it. Take the same approach to reviews as to the initial conversation. Let them have input into where/when the conversation happens (not if) and start by asking them how they think it is going. What has worked well? What hasn't worked well? Why? What have they learnt? Almost certainly there will have been failures (not necessarily because they didn't have good intentions but possibly because their brains got hijacked by their reward centre). Reviews are not an opportunity for you to have a go at them for failing, they are a chance to collaborate to find ways to overcome any obstacles.

Remember, false starts and mistakes are part of the learning cycle. If you have a staunch gamer in your house, then changing their routine isn't really the end point. Completing their homework isn't really the end point. Ultimately, supporting them to move forward is about helping them learn how to self-regulate and motivate themselves toward their own futures. Every time we nudge our teen off their console and out of their room, we create an opportunity for them to find the thread that will lead them into their future.

But there is a big proviso here: your teen has to be able to face that future. If the real reason your teenager has withdrawn to their console is as a coping mechanism to escape low mood or poor wellbeing, just turning off their game won't help. Nudging them toward a positive routine will still be important, but prioritising warmth and connection will be paramount. If your teen's withdrawal into gaming is new or extreme or accompanied by a sudden change in mood, it's definitely worth asking yourself what might be going on under the surface.

CHAPTER 7
HOW TO HELP LIFT A LOW MOOD

It's not uncommon for teens to experience periods of low mood. Being a teenager in today's world is challenging and when your emotional brain regions are so pumped up, the highs can be sky high and the lows really deep. For some teens, low mood can become severe and prolonged, and just opening their curtains (let alone coming out of their room) can feel like too big a step.

Whether your teen is suffering from a diagnosed depression or just having a few bad days, there are lots of things parents can do to reach out and connect. The first challenge is to recognize their low mood – which is harder than it sounds. Parents often mistake teens' low mood symptoms for bad behaviour or mislabel their coping mechanism as the cause. For example, we see them obsessively gaming or scrolling through social media or binging on sugary snacks, and blame these as the root of their problem when actually these might be a coping response, something that is giving them pleasure or helping them fill the hours at a time when they don't feel happy and time feels oppressive.

Looking past teens' behaviour to the thoughts and feelings that might lie behind it can help us stand in their shoes and judge their choices less harshly. When your teen's mood is low, a loving and understanding relationship will be more important than ever. We need to turn down the pressure, turn off the criticism and create a nurturing space for them to feel well again.

What does teenage low mood look like?

When we think of low mood, we typically imagine sadness, maybe tearfulness, or perhaps lethargy and a general disinterest in doing things. If you see those signs in your teenager, especially if they represent a change from their normal selves, then they may be experiencing low mood. You might notice a sudden lack of interest in their usual activities. A severe low mood can manifest as a total lack of energy or motivation to do even simple things around basic self-care or hygiene. There might be physical symptoms, too, such as changes in appetite or sleep patterns.

However, in teenagers it is also common for low mood to be expressed through rudeness, irritability and lashing out. Your teen might retreat behind a wall of silence and indifference, only to react angrily when you challenge them or try to get them to engage. Teens are more likely than adults to display anger as a symptom of low mood or depression – which can make it difficult for parents to spot what is really going on. When low mood manifests through aggressive or disrespectful behaviour, it takes a superhuman parent to look past that behaviour to see the emotions behind it. Most of us are too busy reacting to our teen's appalling attitude to spot the distress behind their actions (only to feel incredibly guilty once we realize what was actually going on beneath the surface).

Procrastination is another classic sign of low mood. Teens might keep putting off their schoolwork or their chores and then get stressed when deadlines are missed (or when a parent gets annoyed about the unwashed dishes). Phones and gaming often play a big role in this procrastination cycle and can make it harder for parents to spot changes in mood. When teens withdraw into tech, that gets in the way of conversation and spending time together – both of which are needed to get a sense of what's really going on for your teen.

When low mood comes out as anger, or laziness, or indifference, it's common for co-parents to have different views on what's going on and how best to respond. One of you might see disobedience and want to counter this with boundaries and consequences, while the other sees low mood or difficult feelings and wants to respond with empathy. Friends and family often pile in with their own views too, perhaps telling you to be tougher with your teen, to lay down the law and stop pandering to them, when what you see is a child who is struggling and is lashing out from stress. The best way to understand what's really going on and how you can help is, of course, to start by talking with your teen.

Is it low mood or depression?

In chapter 9, I'll set out some guidelines on when you should seek help for a teen's mental health (and where to go). But, as a rule of thumb, if your teenager's mood makes sense in the circumstances and they are responding to it in ways which provide them with relief (without doing harm), then that's generally a good sign. They might still need some support, and their feelings might be difficult to experience (and for you to witness) but this probably isn't a mental health disorder.* For example, if your teen has been through a breakup and they are low, tearful and reluctant to engage in their usual activities, that's an appropriate emotional response. If they are listening to sad music, crying, looking

---

* Lisa Damour sums this up brilliantly. "Mental health is not about feeling good. Instead, it's about having the right feelings at the right time and being able to manage those feelings effectively." Lisa Damour, *The Emotional Lives of Teenagers* (Allen & Unwin, 2023).

through old photos, writing poems or going on windy walks to cope with their feelings, those are appropriate non-harmful coping strategies. Hopefully, their hurt will reduce quickly and their mood will lift.

On the other hand, if your teenager seems stuck in a negative state of mind for a prolonged period of time, or in a low mood that has no logical cause, with sadness they can't alleviate, or shows signs of physical changes such as weight loss, or if they report feeling numb or bleak or having feelings of worthlessness or shame and they are finding it hard to manage simple daily tasks, it's more likely to be depression and you should seek professional support. Even if their mood does not seem to you to be so low but they are using harmful coping strategies (such as cutting, drugs, alcohol, or fire-setting), that is a clear sign that their mental health may be compromised. Only a trained mental health professional can diagnose depression, so you will need to seek expert help.

In the meantime, whether this is a short low mood or a more prolonged depression (or you are stuck in limbo waiting for assessment or treatment), the strategies in the next section will help you be the parent your teenager needs to help them find a path back to hopefulness.

A FEW WORDS ABOUT SUICIDE

If you are worried your teenager might be thinking about harming themselves, don't be afraid to ask them directly.

Have you had any really dark thoughts? Maybe thoughts that life isn't worth living? Or thoughts about harming yourself?

If your teen has been thinking about suicide, it will probably be a relief to talk about it. Don't worry that it will somehow give them the idea or put thoughts into their head.

If your teen discloses thoughts of suicide, listen calmly and non-judgementally (catch your shock and hold it still inside for later). Seek support as soon as possible via your child's doctor.

If you think your teenager is at imminent risk of self-harm, take them to the emergency department at your local hospital. (If they are reluctant to go, seek advice from the emergency services.)

Being there for your teenager

Parenting a teen who is struggling with low mood can be lonely and entail a lot of self-doubt. When teens won't talk (or will talk only to you), it's hard to feel confident about your parenting choices. You can't wave a magic wand to fix your teen: their recovery will take its own path. You won't always know the right thing to do or say and you'll frequently feel disheartened when nothing you do seems to work and when each glimmer of a step forward is followed by what feels like a step backward. Your job is to keep showing up no matter what, to keep showing them that you care, to keep showing that you're on their side and that they are not alone, and to hold your relationship open and keep offering connection.

This is the time to let go of policing the rules and be gentle instead. Yes, it would be preferable if your teen would come downstairs and join the family for dinner – but if low mood is making that painful for them, maybe this is the moment to set aside your principles and pop into their room with a healthy plate of food and a smile? There is never just one right way to parent, and if your child is having a hard time engaging with the world or feeling positive, your parenting needs to adapt to that. Helping a down teen feel understood, seen and loved is a truly therapeutic act. This isn't about finding a way to make them better; it's about walking alongside them through the tough times and providing a relationship that feels sturdy enough to support them as they find a way out of this low mood. That means letting them know that we love them unconditionally and that our love is big enough to hold whatever they are feeling.*

How do I do that when my teen won't come out of their bedroom? You'll have to keep nudging at their door. Try to pick your moments wisely to get into their space in a gentle, friendly way. Pop into their room (knock first) to see if they need anything. Or just take them something nice to show them you care (and ignore any scowling). A hot chocolate with whipped cream and marshmallows is an entry ticket into most teen bedrooms. Even if your teen doesn't drink the cocoa, it signals to them that they are loved and that you care. Those little gestures mean a lot. If they are in a conducive mood, you might even be able to linger a little. Maybe sit on their bed and tell them something about your day? This often won't work but sometimes it will, and you'll get to sit with them and have a valuable chat or maybe they'll agree to come out for a bit. Keep trying. Be alert to the best moments and respect their choices. If they vehemently don't want to engage in conversation, withdraw.

It looks like you don't want to talk to me right now. I'll come back later.

By being kind to our teen, we model to them how to be kind to themselves, and signal that that they are worthy of that self-care and compassion. Your gestures of kindness won't always be appreciated. They will often be ignored and, sometimes, when those teenage defences flare up, they will be batted

---

* It is an approach that Suzanne Alderson labels "partnering not parenting" in her wonderful book *Never Let Go: How to Parent Your Child Through Mental Illness* (Vermilion, 2020).

straight back at you with an added helping of scorn. Let the failures pass and try not to get provoked into a reaction. And when it works? When they do smile back, or say thanks, or give you a squeeze and tell you you're the best, remember to cherish those moments and dwell on them. Those little moments are much more important than they seem. Keep on being available and loving. Let them know through small acts of kindness that you like them, care about them and are available to talk if they want to. Even if they don't take you up on the offer, it will still have an impact.

Try to avoid negative messaging (for example, *If you don't buck up and get out of bed, you are going to fall behind and never catch up on your schoolwork*). A teenager who is feeling low is already feeling bad, they don't need to be given more reasons to feel that they are failing. Positive messaging is much more helpful. Lack of hope is a key factor in low mood, so hold that hope for them. That doesn't mean minimizing how awful they are feeling and telling them it's all going to be OK. Use those empathetic listening skills to be the safe listener they can rely on – but also let them know that no matter how hard it feels right now, it won't always feel this way. And that although right now it might be difficult for them to imagine a bright future, that doesn't mean that bright future isn't waiting around the corner.

Rather than calling out their unhelpful habits, gently point out positive patterns.

I've noticed that you seem a bit happier on the days when you get up early.

You seemed to enjoy that walk.

Focusing on small positive steps can help your teen gain a sense of control and agency so celebrate the small wins and brighter moments and try not to assume each positive step will lead to a big leap forward. The route out of low mood is often zigzaggy rather than straight, with bad days following good ones. What works today may not work tomorrow, but keep on trying.

Keep your fears and worries (about their schoolwork, their future, their prospects, etc) out of your interactions with your teenager. Maybe take the pressure off for a couple of days, for a few weeks, for a whole year, whatever is needed. Because let's be clear, there is a hierarchy of what matters here. To succeed (in school, family and life), good mental health is essential. Your teen needs the mental and emotional resources to feel equal to the challenges facing them – and that might not happen on exactly the same schedule as you (or the school system) would like.

Most importantly, try not to offload your own emotions onto a teenager who is struggling to manage theirs (especially if their pain is causing you to become distressed or resurfacing your own past hurts). You certainly won't get every conversation right, and some conversations you'll get badly wrong. When you take a misstep, or vent your frustration, own it as yours. Be honest that your reaction was coming from a place of worry and that it wasn't helpful. Reflect, repair and revisit that conversation a better way another time. And take it as a reminder to prioritize your own self-care and be as kind to yourself as you are trying to be to your teen.

Some useful mood-boosting ideas

We can't fix a teen's mood, but we can support teens to lift their mood by focusing on simple positive lifestyle factors. This isn't about trying prescribing solutions; it's about gently supporting them to try out mood-boosting ideas that might work for them. This needs to be done gently, patiently and without criticism. A mental health practitioner once described this process to me as like pulling on a fragile thread. Imagine a thread of cotton attached to your teen. To encourage them to move in the direction you want them to go, you need to pull on the thread. But if you tug too hard, the thread will break. So, pull gently, and if there is too much resistance, just drop it. Gently, softly persist and, eventually, you will pull a thread and your teen will budge a little. They will agree to go for a walk or to eat a healthy meal or just to pull their curtains and have a shower. And through that experience, they get a little respite from the low mood and maybe a template for how they might find that respite again.

Lots of these threads will go nowhere but try not to be disheartened because you never know where a thread might lead. In the depths of his depression, when his eating was irregular and erratic, my son really liked one (and only one) Thai dish from our local healthy-ish takeaway. So, I pulled that thread often (it was one of many threads I tried!). Usually, he would come downstairs when the food arrived and, although he didn't linger long, there might be a few positive exchanges. I found a Thai cookery book that had the recipe for that dish, so I bought it for him for Christmas. The book sat on the shelf gathering dust but then one day, he said he wanted to try cooking his favourite Thai dish, so I dashed to the shop and got all the ingredients. By the time I got back, he had changed his mind, but a couple of weeks later, we worked through the recipe together. A few weeks after that, he made the dish again and then, eventually, he tried another recipe from the book. Slowly, he discovered a passion for cooking which turned out to be a huge part of his path toward good mental health. We never know which threads will work, or where they might lead.

The mood-boosting ideas below are not offered as guaranteed quick fixes. They will only work if your teen is willing to give them a try – but these are threads worth pulling. These mood-boosters can be helpful whether your teen is just feeling a bit blah or (alongside professional help) if your teen is stuck in a dark place.

Exercise

Lots of teens drop out of the organized sports they played as children, often due to body image concerns, friendship changes or just lack of interest. However, exercise is really good for our mental health. Schoolwork plus spending lots of time in their rooms on digital devices can add up to a pretty sedentary lifestyle for a modern teen, so anything you can do to increase activity levels is likely to be beneficial for their mood.

A teen who is feeling low and who doesn't like sport may not respond well to the suggestion that they join the local volleyball club, so maybe look for opportunities for bite-sized bits of exercise instead. Increased activity levels all add up. Walking to the shop, a keepy-uppy football session in the garden, a 15-minute online yoga or dance class – anything that gets your teen moving is worth encouraging. Every time you head out somewhere, ask if they want to come. They will probably say no but one day they might just say yes (and in the meantime you'll be showing them they are loved and included).

Healthy food

There is growing evidence that the gut impacts mood and wellbeing. Lots of teens develop poor eating habits, especially when they are feeling down, with diets full of chocolate, crisps and fast food. Do whatever you can to squeeze some nutrient-rich food into your teenager. You might need to be creative, especially if they are reluctant to try anything healthy. Remember when you used to sneak fruit and vegetables into their meals as toddlers? Well, if it works, it's worth a try! Think smoothies with Greek yoghurt, probiotics and their favourite fruit (with a blob of honey if required to make it more acceptable), or blended soups or pasta sauces with hidden greens. Be prepared to compromise. Ideals are all well and good for perfect situations but getting nutrients into a depressed teen with a poor diet usually involves compromises to kickstart a change.

Remember, every time you pop into their room with a fruit juice and a banana, it's also a micro-act of love and kindness. You can't badger or reason a depressed teen into eating better, but you can put a plate of food in front of them with a smile or a kiss on their forehead (and take it away again with the same spirit if it isn't eaten). Even if that banana goes brown on their bedside table or the offer is point-blank refused, keep trying.

(As a side note, as I write this, I can hear my no-longer-a-teen in the kitchen blending up a smoothie. As I said, it's a long game and you never know where each thread will lead . . .)

Get out into nature

If your teen isn't sleeping well or is spending a lot of time in their bedroom, getting out into daylight will help reset their circadian rhythm. If your teen's low mood is prolonged and preventing them from going about daily life, try to nudge them to get outside. Even a few minutes in nature helps to boost mood, so encourage your teen to get out into some greenery if you can. Be creative. Big, small, whatever works. Walk the dog in the woods, drive to the coast to walk on the beach in winter, or just sit on a bench in your yard.

Exposure to early daylight is thought to be especially helpful for resetting regular sleep/rising patterns. I know (I can hear your eyes rolling!), persuading a teenager out of their bed early in the morning is a gargantuan challenge, but perhaps just sneak into their room to open one curtain (and hope that inertia stops them getting out of bed to close it again!).

Sleep

If your teen's mood is low, they might be sleeping too much, sleeping too little or sleeping at all the wrong times. We know that good sleep hygiene (such as going to bed at the same time every day and not using devices late at night) can help promote positive sleep routines, but when teens are low, they usually have the opposite of good sleep habits. And when they are not sleeping well, the impacts on their mood (and appetite and wellbeing) can be enormous.

Rather than prescribing a solution they won't implement, collaborate with your teen on what helps and be open to exploring ideas with them. What have they tried so far when they can't sleep? What might improve their sleep quality? Be gentle and curious (there is nothing more infuriating to a person who can't sleep than being told what they are getting wrong). Collaborate to come up with a list of ideas to try. Some parents report success with the aid of weighted blankets, white noise or meditation.

If your teen is really low, and especially if you are concerned about self-harm, make sure they know you are available if they need you in the middle of the night. Difficult thoughts and feelings can come crowding in when teens are awake alone late at night. Many parents of depressed teens will tell of nights sat with their teen when things were really bad, talking to them to keep the thoughts away, or just stroking their hair.

Gratitude

This might be as simple as writing down three good things that have happened that day or spending a few moments thinking about the brightest moments of the day. You can buy positive psychology journals that will encourage your teen toward gratitude and help them to set positive intentions for the next day. But a simple notebook, or just a one-minute conversation with you modelling the process and identifying your three best moments, is a great place to start. If the day has been really bleak, find a joint happy memory to talk about.

Humour

Laughter is a great mood-booster. Show them that picture of their baby cousin with chocolate cake on their face, encourage them to watch a funny programme on TV – notice whatever raises the flicker of a smile and brings a bit of respite from their low mood (and try to do more of it). Laughter isn't easy to find when mood is low, but moments of lightness are brilliant for giving respite, creating connection and helping teens feel accepted – which will make the rest of these mood-boosting ideas much more achievable.

Imagining

In those small moments when your teen seems open to connecting, when they let you, engage them in imagination.

I'm thinking about painting the kitchen, what colour do you think might work?

If you had unlimited money, where would you go on holiday?

Where's the most beautiful place you have ever been?

Take the pressure off and keep things hypothetical by talking about things other than them and their real problems. Just being able to spend some time thinking about something light and different can bring relief. And when we use our imagination, it also can create a sense of possibilities, hope and even goals.

Cosy up

There are times when a bit of *hygge* is the best medicine: cosy slippers, a hot drink, snuggled up under blankets for your favourite TV programme. If your teen is not coming out of their room, see if you can work with them to cosy up their bedroom a little. Maybe offer a new rug or lamp or pot plant (or just a clean duvet cover!). Some people are especially sensitive to their environment (lighting, textures, etc) and although our aim is to get our teen out of their bedroom, if low mood is leading them to spend a lot of time in there, then boosting their mood through a more pleasant environment might be worth a try.

Whichever of these threads you choose to pull, try not to get too attached to any one idea or suggestion. If you invest all your parental hopes in that pot plant, you're going to take a big hit when it dies from lack of sunlight or gets knocked over and is left roots-up on the floor. This isn't about you finding ways to fix your teen's mood (as much as you want to do that), it's about treating them with love, care and respect and creating a nurturing environment so that they can find ways to build themselves up and discover the steps that will take them to a more positive place.

CHAPTER 8
BUILDING YOUR TEENAGER'S CONFIDENCE

If we want to get teenagers out of their bedrooms and help them to thrive as young adults, then building their confidence is key. Worries and self-doubt can be huge barriers to a teen's transition to independence and make it far more likely that they will retreat to the sanctuary of their rooms. The teenage years are naturally a period of acute self-consciousness. As those independence drives kick in (and sexuality starts to bloom), concerns around fitting in and body image are ubiquitous, and many teens experience higher levels of anxiety at this stage than at any other time in their lives. Even children who were confident and outgoing in their younger years can become withdrawn or unsure of themselves as teenagers. When your brain is sending signals that the world is a threatening place, retreating to the safety of your bedroom is a logical step.

The good news is that over time most teens succeed in overcoming their worries and self-doubt and become more secure in themselves. Their brains mature and balance is restored between their emotional threat-detecting limbic system and their more rational prefrontal cortex. They experience moments of success and start to believe in themselves a bit more. And, gradually, as they move into young adulthood, they identify their strengths and passions and start to build a life around them. This is a journey that proceeds at different rates for different teens (and seldom in a straight line). Having a positive relationship with an adult who believes in them is a huge facilitating factor.

However, for some teens, anxiety and lack of confidence can become major obstacles on this journey. Rather than experiencing success and finding their feet, anxious teens often withdraw from situations they find difficult and lose belief in their ability to face fears and challenges. Their world starts to shrink rather than expand, and their threat-alert amygdala sees danger at every step. This anxiety might manifest as a generalized sense of unease or self-criticism, or through more extreme responses such as school refusal, restricted eating, or panic attacks. And parents can feel powerless to help. We see the happy, confident child they were and wonder what has gone wrong. We see their worry but can't reason it away. We strive to build up their confidence by telling them how wonderful they are, but it makes no difference. Or maybe we lose patience and tell them to get over it (but that doesn't help either).

For teens to develop confidence, they need to experience moments to shine. These are the moments when they feel a sense of pride or triumph that they have achieved something difficult or made a difference in some way. These are moments that extend their skills and their self-belief and that take them to the edge of what they can manage (but without being so difficult that they become disheartened and give up). Building confidence involves challenging ourselves and being brave, and that can be a big hurdle for a teen who is overcome by worries and clinging to their comfort zone.

What is anxiety?

Feeling worried, alarmed, stressed or anxious is perfectly normal. We all feel that way sometimes. Indeed, anxiety is a helpful part of normal brain functioning. Anxiety is a bit like an early warning system that gets us ready to respond efficiently to challenges, threat or danger. When we perceive a threat, our brains prime us with energy and resources to help us through that situation and protect ourselves from harm. If there is an escaped tiger on the loose in your garden, an anxious alarm response is exactly what you need to make sure you stay alert and alive. Even if it is just a sports match or a test in class that you're facing, the extra capabilities and nervous energy released by your anxious brain will quicken your responses so you can perform better.

However, problems can arise when our anxious response is out of proportion to the scale of the threat. For example, if you feel panicky and full of fear every time you step outside the house when there is no cause for alarm (and no tiger!), that's less useful. Anxiety becomes unhelpful when it gets in the way of us doing things that we need to do or that we want to do, and when it hinders everyday life.

When we're experiencing anxiety, it usually feels like everything inside is happening all at once. But break it down and an anxious response is actually made up of three parts:

- **Cognitive element**: the thoughts whirring through our mind as we face (or imagine facing) a difficult situation. These are the words in your head. For example, an anxious teenager might be thinking "I'm going to fail" or "People will laugh at me" or "I look stupid".
- **Physiological element**: the changes that happen in our body when we feel anxious or worried. For example, your teenager might sweat, breathe rapidly or feel nauseous. They might blush.
- **Behavioural element**: what we do when we feel anxious. An anxious teenager might lock themselves in the bathroom, cry, yell or lash out and try to get away from whatever is triggering their alarm (or avoid going into that situation).

Anxiety doesn't affect everyone equally – both nature and nurture play a part here. Some people are born with a more anxious temperament than others. Some people have a more reactive nervous system, and naturally have a lower threshold for tolerating new situations. For some people, a traumatic or stressful event might trigger anxiety or programme their nervous system to respond in certain ways. People can learn an anxious response gradually via the people around them or their own experiences.

Teens are especially prone to anxiety, and particularly to social anxiety, because the amygdala (the part of the brain that governs this threat response) is so dominant during the teenage years. Remember all that brain science in chapter 1? The teenage brain is hyperalert to social threats (such as being left out, being humiliated or not fitting in). Teens are acutely aware of how they are perceived, and this coincides with a period in which they are also undergoing rapid changes in their bodies and developing sexual desires. Wanting to be liked and found attractive are natural psychological components in teenage development but it does mean that teens are more vulnerable to worrying about what people think of them and feeling insecure. Self-acceptance and self-confidence are simply more difficult when you are a teenager.

However, this psychological and neurological predisposition to insecurity doesn't mean that all teenage anxiety is problematic. With most teens, it's probably more helpful to think of anxiety as a basket term which includes a wide range of agitated states – such as feeling nervous, or worried, or apprehensive, or even excited. Teens tend to experience these states with the dial turned up (due their souped-up limbic regions) which can be uncomfortable and sometimes distressing. But learning to manage uncomfortable thoughts and feelings, and finding ways to direct their behaviour appropriately so they can respond positively, is part of a teen's journey to becoming an independent young adult. It is emotional learning they must go through for themselves, and we can't short-circuit it for them (no matter how much we might wish to).

Some teens do develop severe anxiety disorders (which need to be clinically diagnosed and treated) in which the anxiety response they experience is so overwhelming it impedes normal teenage activities like leaving the house, going to school or being home alone. Neurodiverse teens are especially prone to higher levels of anxiety. When teens have ADHD that is not diagnosed or well controlled, the teenage years can be a particularly turbulent time. It is also a time when late diagnosis of autism (especially in girls) is common, with acute anxiety issues often being a trigger for ASD assessment.

Helping teens find their bravery

Whether your teen is experiencing a temporary blip in self-confidence or a more prolonged struggle with anxiety, parents often feel quite lost as to how to respond to a worried or panicky teen, especially one who has hunkered down in their bedroom and won't face the world. Usually, we cycle through a range of strategies. We try reassuring them that it's all going to be okay and telling them not to worry. We offer them ideas on what they should do and how to handle the situation. We try being gentle and empathizing. When that doesn't shift them, we might get tough and try to force them to face their fears. Then, when they are really upset, we might give in and allow them to stay in their room. Next time, we try it all again, circling through different responses, getting more and more frustrated and emotional ourselves.

Why won't they just give it a go? There's nothing to be scared of! If you have never experienced low self-confidence or high levels of anxiety, it can be truly baffling to understand why your teen can't join that rowing club or speak to that shop assistant or just do the things that other teens are doing. Our instinct is often to try and reason them out of their worries.

Your friends will be there, you'll have fun. There's nothing to worry about.

The mismatch between our rational assessment of the situation and our teen's fear makes no sense. It might even strike you as stubbornness. You might feel annoyed that your teen is wasting opportunities. Or you might feel a sense of shame that they are not stepping up to society's expectations. Unfortunately, telling a worried teen not to worry is seldom effective.

On the other hand, if you have experienced anxiety yourself (or remember it powerfully as a teenager), a common reaction is to shield our children and help them feel safe. We understand how they feel, and it starts to trigger that feeling in us too, deep in the pit of our stomachs. We imagine being them, feeling humiliated or stared at. We lie awake at night worrying about how we can protect them.

That's fine, sweetheart, you don't need to go, I know how hard this is for you, I'll tell them you're not well today.

We love our teens and would do anything to take their pain away. But, by shielding them, they stay stuck in their fears.

The most effective way parents can support teens to build their confidence is to help them to find the bravery inside themselves, so they can rise to the challenges they face and grow their own belief in their ability to succeed. Your unique and wonderful teen might lack the confidence to step out of their room for any number of reasons. They might have specific worries (like acne), or concerns triggered through past experiences, or more generalized levels of clinical anxiety (which will need professional support). Your role remains the same: to support them to find and use their own bravery in pursuit of some success and moments to shine.

There is no magic spell for helping a teen feel brave, this is trial and error stuff. But whatever the journey looks like for your teen, these four principles will guide you through:

- Believe in them
- Avoid avoidance
- Build coping skills
- Encourage small brave steps.

Believe in them

When it comes to unconfident or anxious teens, our number one job is to hold firm to the belief that our teen is equal to the challenges facing them, and to signal that to them clearly so they can believe it too. Belief is contagious. By having faith in our teen's bravery and resilience, we gift a little of that belief to them. That doesn't mean minimizing or dismissing their fears or worries – these are absolutely real to them. You'll need to use all those empathetic listening skills we looked at in chapter 5.

I can see you're really worried. This feels like an impossible task right now. But I believe you can make progress.

While acknowledging how big the challenge feels to them, we should always convey that we believe they are capable of finding a way forward.

In essence, this comes down to having positive expectations. That can be especially hard if recent experience has led you to expect wobbles and failures rather than success. For example, if a teen has struggled on sleepovers in the past and these have ended in tears, with fraught phone calls and late-night dashes to pick them up, then a parent will naturally feel a bit nervous when another sleepover comes around. We might ask them how they are feeling about it in a worried voice (or maybe ask once too often). We might reassure them repeatedly that it will be OK (while sending the message that we are not confident they can manage it).

> *Sam's mum is really nice. She'll look out for you, just tell her if you're feeling worried. It's not far away so I can always come pick you up, if necessary, just call me.*

And, you know, maybe they won't manage this sleepover. But repeated negative expectations will make that more likely, not less.

When we underestimate our teen's capacity to meet a challenge, they can learn to underestimate themselves too. We want our teens to believe that no matter how scary or difficult a challenge might be, they are equal to it. It might be hard. They might not manage it this time, but they are equal to this challenge, and they will get there. And every time they try is a valuable step on that journey.

Avoid avoidance

Avoiding a situation that makes you anxious is a natural and logical response. In the short term, avoidance works brilliantly. Anxiety is not a pleasant state. If your teen is wound up to fever pitch about going to school and you agree that they can stay home for the day, they are going to experience a huge sense of relief. Their anxiety levels are going to drop. But what does their brain learn from that avoidance for the future? Your teen learns that the best way to feel calm is to stay at home and avoid school. (They may also learn that the more distressed they become, and the worse their behaviour, the more likely we are to allow them stay home!). The prospect of leaving their room and going to school the next day provokes even more distress, and the only way they have learned to reduce that distress is not to go to school.

In the long term, avoiding anxiety-triggering situations escalates anxiety and reduces confidence. It shrinks teens' worlds, narrows their experiences, and makes it even harder for them to believe in their capacity to face a difficult situation. So, it's essential that parents don't allow teens to see avoidance as the solution. That's not to say that we force a teen who is in the grip of a panic attack out of the door, but that we are always on the lookout for opportunities to move them toward their fears (albeit in small, supported steps) rather than keeping them away from them.

> *I can see you're in a total panic. Why don't you take a moment to sit still and breathe and calm yourself down. Once you feel calmer, we'll have a think about what might help you feel more able to face school.*

Our aim is to help them stretch their capacity to tolerate anxious moments and help them face difficult situations, rather than removing the source of their anxiety completely.

Avoiding avoidance is not always easy. You might find yourself in the firing line of some cruel angry words if you refuse to give way and do what your teen wants. An anxious teen can go to extreme lengths to avoid the source of their distress, and that includes aggression, lies and deceit. For example, you might be told that their class was cancelled, or the bus was late or that they stayed at home to redo their assignment because the school computer system lost it, when actually your teen is avoiding class because being in that group situation sets off their panic alarm. You might be dropping them off at the school gate and watching them walk in, for them just to turn around and walk out as soon as you drive away. We can't force a teen to take on a challenge but, as a principle, whenever you can, avoid facilitating their avoidant behaviour.

PERSONAL STORY

ONE OF MY BETTER PARENTING MOMENTS!

Teen: Mum, please can you phone work and tell them I'm sick. I can't go in

Me: How come?

Teen: I hate it. I don't want to go.

Me: I hear you. I sometimes don't want to go to work. Is there a particular reason you especially don't feel like it today?

Teen: I just don't feel like it. Phone them and tell them I'm sick.

Me: I'm not going to phone your manager and lie to her just because you don't feel like going.

Teen: Alex is off today which means I will have to fill in on the food counter. I hate standing there with everyone watching me. I always make mistakes and I can feel all the college kids looking at me. I can't go in. I feel sick, I'm not joking.

Me: Yeah, I can see that. I know it makes you uncomfortable when you have to deal with customers, and you'd rather avoid that. I feel for you. But I'm not going to phone them and tell them you're sick. You are going to have to find another way to manage this situation.

Teen: There isn't another way, I'm just not going. If I lose my job, it's your fault!

Me: Well, losing your job is also an option. I'm not sure it's the best option, though, so you might want to think of a different approach. I'm pretty sure no matter how hard this feels, you'll find a way through it.*

---

* If you are curious, the upshot in this case was a lot of slammed doors followed by a last-minute lift to work conducted in hostile silence. This one didn't end in tears.

Build coping skills

If you are going to discourage avoidance and insist (albeit gently) that your teen faces their fears, they will need some strategies for calming themselves and coping with the flood of thoughts and feelings that can accompany challenging moments. Your teen won't be able to find their bravery if they are completely overwhelmed.

To decelerate an anxious response and find calm, we can utilize any one of the three components of anxiety – mind, body or behaviour. For example, there might be words that your teenager could say to themselves that have a calming effect and make them feel more confident. Or they might find ways to calm their body through breathing or exercise. Or they might use habits and routines to make difficult moments more manageable (such as walking to school with a friend).

Unfortunately, teens often don't take kindly to parents prying into their thoughts or telling them how they should do things (our advice tends to land as criticism). They are far more likely to engage positively in that discussion with a therapist or a counsellor. When it comes to coping skills, it's often more effective for parents to assume the role of supportive helper rather than expert advisor. Questions which draw on your teen's own knowledge and expertise can be really helpful here. For example, if you want to encourage your teen to replace the negative words in their head with positive ones, you might ask:

What would you say to a friend who was having those thoughts? Could you say that to yourself?

If you want to encourage them to use a relaxation strategy, you might ask:

Is there something that has helped in the past to get rid of that tight feeling in your chest?

If you want to encourage them to come up with a fallback plan:

What's your plan for getting through it if you do feel a bit jittery at the sleepover?

Rather than giving advice, you might ask them for solutions.

What might make you feel a bit better about going?

These types of questions are less threatening to a teen's independence so a little less likely to provoke a defensive response. They also hand the problem back to our teen in a way that signals to them that, although we are here to support them, we believe they are equal to the task of solving this problem for themselves.

Of course, your teen might still spit this support back at you. Or try to coerce you into rescuing them. Be prepared to allow them to sit with their own discomfort or, if their anxiety is coming out as aggression, to walk away kindly.

I can see you're too upset to talk about this right now. I'll leave you to calm down and I'll come back in a few minutes.

If they do try out a coping strategy, be encouraging, even if it doesn't work.

Well done for trying it. That was a really positive step.

And if they reach for harmful coping strategies, such as alcohol or weed, try to be understanding about where that might be coming from while you draw a boundary.

I totally understand why the weed is tempting. It takes away the whizzing thoughts and makes you feel calm. But it also has serious negative risks, and I can't stand by and allow you to harm yourself in that way. I wonder what else you could do that might be calming but is healthier?

Remember, the coping strategies that work for you might not work for your teen. Encourage them to explore different ways to bring down their agitated thoughts and feelings to the level where their brain's response supports them to be brave rather than sends them running for cover.

ACTION POINT

Encourage your teen to research strategies for coping with worries and anxious moments. Point them toward quality resources (see the Resources for Parents at the end of this book for ideas).

They might find it helpful to look up:

- Relaxation techniques – eg breathing strategies
- Mindfulness – eg guided meditation apps
- Worry strategies – eg using a worry book
- Positive self-talk – eg coping statements.

Remember, the coping strategies that you find helpful may not work for your teen, and they may have to try different approaches before finding something that helps them.

Encourage small brave steps

The more often your teenager can step out of their bedroom to face an anxiety-provoking situation and find a way through it (without running away) then start to feel calm again, the easier it will be for them to have confidence in themselves and the greater their capacity to face that situation again in the future. Our brains learn through experience, and the teenage brain is primed for learning. We want teens to experience success in rising to the challenge of their own fears and worries. Having some coping skills to help them through unconfident or worried moments will definitely help, but if their fears are too great, asking your teen to face a situation all in one go might be too much. In which case, breaking things down into smaller steps can be helpful.

For example, if your teen is nervous about auditioning for the school band, ask them which parts of the process worry them most and which worry them least. Look for some small wins by tackling the least worrying bits first. If playing in front of peers is the difficult bit, they could build their confidence by performing their audition piece to the mirror in the first instance, then to family members and then to one trusted friend. Or start with recording it and playing it to one person. If your teen lacks confidence to join a new club or team, they might start off by being a spectator or just chatting to the coach on their own.

Ideally, these smaller steps require them to be brave but in slightly more manageable doses than standing up on stage or jumping straight in. At each step, your teen can use their coping skills to help, for example by taking deep breaths or using a coping statement to manage their thoughts (*"I have done hard things before"* is a great one – but let your teen choose words that work for them). Your teen might want to write down some reassuring words on a card and keep that in their pocket to look at if needed.

If we can support our teens to face situations that make them anxious in small steps, they can practise overcoming fear and lack of confidence and experience a little glimmer of success. More importantly, their brain will learn that they are capable of feeling unsure or worried but overcoming that. They can feel the fear but do it anyway, which is the foundation of confidence.

There is no forcing a teen to do any of this. We can only encourage them and celebrate each positive step with them. For some teens, it is a long road to finding a sense of success and confidence in themselves. And, if their anxiety is acute, it might be slow progress with lots of looping back as well as inching forward. But independence isn't a race. Really, it isn't.

CHAPTER 9
WHEN TO WORRY

When a teenager retreats to their bedroom, it is usually temporary and transitional and nothing to worry about. However, sometimes teen withdrawal can be a sign that there is something going on that might need professional support. It is not always easy to distinguish normal changes in teenage moods from the types of changes that indicate a teen is seriously struggling. And if your teen has pushed you away, it can be even harder to know what's going on inside them. The more you can implement the strategies in this book – to build relationship, stand in their shoes, and keep communication channels open – the more likely you are to pick up on any worrying signs (and the more willing your teen will be to disclose them).

There is a fine line between a teenager who is feeling all the feelings but coping, and one who is struggling with all their feelings and not coping. Teenagers feel everything intensely. Their emotional states are highly charged. Their moods are often erratic, their energy levels and sleep patterns are frequently off-kilter and they are prone to making poor decisions. That's part and parcel of the teenage developmental stage. But these same signs of just "being a teenager" might also be symptoms of poor mental health, or indicators of bullying, substance misuse or disordered eating, so it's vital that you keep an open mind. Our ability to detect when a teenager needs support always starts with our willingness to be curious and look deeper into their behaviour.

If you are looking at your teen's outbursts and poor attitude and dismissing these as disrespectful or entitled, you may be right. But be careful not to close your mind to other possibilities. Could they be acting bad on the outside because they are feeling bad on the inside? Are they lashing out from shame or anxiety? Could their negative attitude be a sign of low mood or poor self-esteem rather than deliberate antagonism? Most teens will bounce through their turbulent teenage years and blossom into lovely, balanced, polite and respectful young adults. But teens are vulnerable and it's essential that, as parents, we remain curious about what lies behind their behaviour rather than just reacting to it.

Warning signs to look out for

You know your child best so trust your instincts. If your teen's behaviour and emotions just don't add up to you, it's time to think hard and dig deeper. Be alert to changes in patterns of behaviour and, especially, to these red flags:

- Physical symptoms such as recurrent stomach aches, headaches, appetite changes, weight loss, sleep problems, loss of energy, fatigue
- Loss of interest in things they used to enjoy, sadness, not enjoying life, lethargy, continuous low mood
- Lack of concentration, sudden drops in school performance
- Volatile behaviour, including irritability, lashing out, sensitivity to criticism, extreme perfectionism, emotional outburst.
- Being tense, fidgety, agitated, fearful or panicky, with breathlessness or sweating.
- Social isolation, reduced friendships, withdrawing socially

- Repeated risky or reckless behaviour
- Not seeing your teen eat, disordered eating, extreme dieting or obsessive exercising
- Expressing feelings of bleakness, worthlessness or hopelessness
- Using self-destructive or harmful coping mechanisms (such as self-harm or alcohol/drugs).

Be especially concerned when you can see clusters of these red flags. Mental illnesses are more likely to emerge in the adolescent years than at any other life stage. These can be triggered by stressful events, traumatic experiences or adverse family factors. But mental ill-health can also come out of the blue so stay curious about what might be driving your teen's mood or behaviour even if you can see no logical reason for them to be struggling and no obvious trigger.

When to seek help

In general, the time to seek help is when your teen is struggling to access the same opportunities or to participate in the same activities as their peer group. For example, when they won't join in school trips (or go to school at all) because they get too anxious. Or when they are struggling to manage normal daily tasks that we would expect from all teens.

It might be helpful to consider the *persistence* of the problem (how long it has been going on), the *severity* of the problem and the *coping mechanisms* your teen is using.

- **Persistence**: all teens go through ups and downs. However, if your teen seems stuck in a down for more than two weeks, that might indicate a mood disorder.
- **Severity**: many teens retreat to their rooms, but most have some contact with friends outside school (even if only via digital devices). When their withdrawal tips over into social

isolation, and they have no social contacts, that would be concerning.

- **Coping mechanisms**: if your teen is using a harmful coping mechanism such as self-harm (eg cutting or bruising) or alcohol/drugs, this is a cause for concern.

If your teen's symptoms are recent and have a logical cause (for example, they are anxious about impending exams, a college interview or a first date) and they are not preventing them from going about normal life, then use the tools in this book to support them to develop some helpful coping strategies. But if they are using harmful coping mechanisms, or if the problem persists or impacts their ability to manage daily tasks, you should seek professional help.

Encouraging your teen to seek help

Unfortunately, even if you think your teen needs help, they might not want to seek it. There could be lots of reasons for this. Teens often worry that they will be forced to disclose difficult or shameful thoughts and feelings if they agree to talk to a counsellor. Your teen might worry that seeking help means there is something wrong with them. Or maybe their mood is sitting so heavily on them that they don't believe anything will help.

There are no shortcuts to persuading a reluctant teen to seek professional help. As always, you will need to start with a supportive conversation. You will need to be that safe listener who can acknowledge where they are coming from but gently nudge them in a helpful direction.* Remember, offers of support can land like criticisms in the teenage brain, so take care to create a space for them to talk to you and not

---

* You might want to go back and reread chapter 5, especially the section on empathetic listening, if you are struggling to communicate over this issue.

feel judged. It might be helpful to wonder out loud and to be tentative in your suggestions to avoid a defensive response.

I don't know, I'm not you, but I wonder whether getting some help might be a way of taking back some control over your feelings, so you have a bit of calm to think?

If you can point to examples of other young people, or perhaps celebrities that your teen admires, who have recovered from mental health challenges with professional support, that can sometimes be influential. Younger teens place a lot of value on the opinions of other teenagers, so consider whether there is an older teen who might be able to have a discussion with them.

There will be times when parents have to make decisions and insist. However, a therapeutic intervention is much more likely to be successful if a teenager engages positively with it. So, if your teen is dead set against a talking therapy but is willing to try a mindfulness or meditation app, maybe start there. Then, collaborate and build on that to find the next step forward, perhaps using the promise of a reward as encouragement. Remember to hold out lots of hope for them. Remind them that somewhere, around the corner, is a future them who has learnt to manage these difficult thoughts and feelings. They might not be able to imagine that future self right now, but seeking some professional support could help them work out which direction to travel to look for a happier them.

Where to find help

Your first port of call if you are looking for support for your teen is their school and/or your primary healthcare provider (for example, your family doctor). Your teen's school will definitely need to be involved if bullying is part of the problem.

They may also offer support with other issues through an in-house counsellor or a pastoral support teacher who can provide therapeutic help or who can signpost you to relevant local professionals or services. Your family doctor will be able to make an initial mental health assessment and refer your teenager to a specialist clinician, if needed.

Some schools and primary health care providers are absolutely fantastic at responding to teens and to mental health concerns, others less so. Consider writing down all your concerns before having a first discussion with a professional. You will probably be feeling emotional, and this gives you a chance to order your thoughts before the appointment. There is nothing wrong with being emotional when you are talking about something so important, but it can get in the way of you explaining clearly why you are concerned (and it might upset your teenager if they are also present). So, choose a quiet moment to write everything down beforehand. Then, once you are calmer, summarize that into some clear examples or bullet points of why you are worried and take that with you to the appointment. Depending on your teen's age (and the nature of the concerns), they might be seen alone by a clinician but make sure you have an opportunity to present your concerns so that this external perspective can also be taken into account. If you (or your teen) do not get taken seriously, or do not get a supportive response, do not give up, go elsewhere.

Other parents can be a good source of information as to what services are available locally but always bear in mind that their experiences will be unique to them. You will also find some online sources of support in the Resources for Parents section at the back of this book. If your teenager is at risk of harming themselves, always take them straight to your local hospital emergency department.

Looking after you

Supporting a teenager who is struggling, especially a teenager with a mental health disorder, is stressful and can be traumatic. Many parents find that their own mental health is negatively impacted too. The shock of finding out that your child is unwell is immense (especially if they are having negative thoughts about harming themselves), and if you have been misreading their symptoms as simply disobedient or obnoxious, there will probably be a heap of self-blame to process too. The path through teenage mental health challenges is seldom straight. There are frequent ups and downs, and progress can be slow and hard to detect. Positive steps forward tend to be followed by gut-punching relapses. Parents' lives often get put on hold as plans are disrupted by unpredictable crises and just never knowing what the day will hold. Teenage mental illness envelopes the whole family and can take away choices, control, stability, pleasure and precious family experiences.

To be there for a teen who is struggling, you will need to be there for yourself too. You will need to consciously direct energy into looking after yourself as well as your teen. Nurturing your health and wellbeing will make a big difference, even in small doses. Focus on daily acts of self-care – like regular exercise, healthy eating and communicating with friends – and model that self-kindness to your teenager too. You might feel isolated from friends and family who don't understand what's going on but try not to offload your worries onto your teenager. You might find it helpful to seek some cognitive behavioural therapy to manage your thoughts and feelings, especially if your head is whirring with catastrophic thoughts.

Remember, you don't have to get every conversation right, you don't have to have answers, but you will need to keep showing up for your teen and that takes huge reserves of strength and calm. So, find ways to replenish your own cup so you can keep filling theirs.

A TEENAGE GIRL SPEAKS

The label of mental illness isn't what bothered me, it was the fact that I couldn't get out of bed. I couldn't shower, I couldn't speak, and I just didn't care about anything anymore. I was absolutely exhausted.

Mental illness not only ruined my life but also affected everyone in my family too. Sitting here writing this now I can't even begin to imagine the depressive cave I created for my family to live in, and I am thankful for my recovery.

When I look at my friends, almost all of them have some sort of mental health problem – whether that's low self-esteem, anxiety, body image or disordered eating. Why is everyone in my generation struggling? I don't know the answer but all the reasons I see revolve around pressure, comparison and critique.

I think parents get confused about the best way to deal with the mental health of their teens. I'm no expert, but the biggest complaint I hear from my friends is when they express negative thoughts to their parents and they are met with "You're just really emotional and sensitive" or "Don't be so dramatic, it'll all be fine when you go back to school tomorrow."

Please don't say these things. It takes courage to express feelings and show weakness. Dismissing your teen's feelings is never going to help.

Work with your teenager, don't battle her. Being proactive is so much better than a confrontational and tense argument or simply ignoring it. Nobody wants these scary thoughts but, unfortunately, in our generation they come when you hit your teen years.

So, don't judge. Help them find positive coping mechanisms. Be the agony aunt and lifeboat to your child.

CONCLUSION

I won't pretend that implementing the ideas I have outlined in this book will be easy. Or that these tools will instantly fix everything. Parenting teens requires patience and heroic powers of self-management. It is a tightrope walk between giving them space and staying close. It can be joyful one moment and hurtful the next. And it takes time (and mistakes) to learn to stay calm and balanced despite our teen's moods and big emotions (and despite our own fears and feelings).

Parenting is not something we get right. It's an act of trying, of a thousand judgement calls. We seldom feel sure we have done the right thing. But if you can remember (most of the time) to model the behaviour you want your teen to copy, rather than following their lead into conflict, you'll be on a good track. If you can challenge yourself to hand over power and treat your teen with the respect they crave (despite childish responses or immature decision-making), you'll be helping them to move forward. And if you can remember to be curious about what lies behind their behaviour and hold fast to the belief that no matter what you see there, the solution will be found through relationship, not antagonism, you'll be well set.

When teens withdraw to their bedrooms, it's all too easy to get sucked into a cycle of escalating conflict and withdrawal. Rather than adding more fuel to that fire, our job is to look for opportunities to generate goodwill and make it as easy as possible for them to turn back to us. We need to nurture every micro-moment of connection and pick up every crumb of relationship. And we are much more likely to find those moments of connection if we can pull back from criticism, step around teen defensiveness and reduce the threat that our love and closeness poses to their drive for independence. Teens don't need us to add to their negative self-commentary. They need us to show them that despite all their self-doubt, their mistakes, their emotional meltdowns, we still hold them in positive regard and cherish them.

We can't take away all our teens' difficult experiences or big emotions, but we can try to be calm and present in the face of their torrents and hold a safe space for them to experience their disappointments. We can listen, and just be there. When everything else feels turbulent, we need to be their anchor. Their rock. Their stability. There for them, no matter what.

And that means managing our own emotions really well. Not being triggered into anger or guilt or shame by our powerlessness. Remembering that their behaviour is a symptom of their transition, not a reflection of our success or failure as parents. Trying not to let fear or worry or comparisons drive our parenting responses. Parenting teens isn't really about managing our teenagers, it's about managing ourselves. Because it is only when we manage our own emotions that we can hold a safe space for our teens to learn to manage theirs.

None of this is easy. We need to be resilient and optimistic. To acknowledge our own needs, and find ways of meeting those, especially in those times when it feels like our child has wandered way off track or just doesn't love us anymore. Now is the time for radical self-care. Not self-care that is appended as an afterthought, an if-I-have-time option, but front and centre in our daily lives. Because without that radical self-care, we can't provide the emotional stability that makes our teens feel safe. So, be kind to yourself, just as you are kind to your teen, despite your mistakes. And keep believing in a positive future, in the lovely young adult your teen will become, and the love that will once more flow freely.

It might be hard, but I know for absolute certain that you are equal to this task. Because you are reading this book – which means you care, and you are trying. It's the trying that matters most. Your teen sees you trying. No matter how many mistakes you think you have made, your relationship with your teenager is still there to be found and grown. Doing your best doesn't mean you get it all right, it means you keep on trying and you keep on believing in them.

Don't underestimate how powerful it is just to keep on believing in your teens, especially at those times when they are finding it hardest to believe in themselves. If we can hold on to the belief that it won't always be like this – that they will come through whatever challenge they are facing – we signal an absolute faith in them that is deeply therapeutic and transformative. Keep looking for the positives, keep building bridges, enjoy the ups (no matter how tiny) and slowly, over time, the ups will become more frequent. And there will come a day when your teen has shed their awkward skin and is ready to meet you with eyes of love and a true appreciation of everything you have given.

RESOURCES FOR PARENTS

Online

Action for Happiness (global): inspiration for small actions to increase daily wellbeing (www.actionforhappiness.org)

Anxiety Canada (Canada): resources, apps and programmes for adults, teens and children for managing anxiety (www.anxietycanada.com)

Calm Harm (global): an app for teenagers who are self-harming (available via your app store or https://calmharm.co.uk)

Child Mind Institute (USA): provides information and advice for children and families struggling with mental health disorders (www.childmind.org)

Smiling Mind (Australia): resources for supporting healthy minds in children, teens and adults (www.smilingmind.com.au)

Triple P Fear-Less Online (global): online course for parents of children (6–14yrs) experiencing anxiety (www.triplep-parenting.net)

Young Minds (UK): advice and support for parents and teens on mental and emotional health issues (www.youngminds.org.uk)

Books

Alderson, Suzanne, *Never Let Go: How to Parent Your Child Through Mental Illness* (Vermilion, 2020)

Candy, Lorraine, *"Mum, What's Wrong With You?": 101 Things Only Mothers of Teenage Girls Know* (4th Estate, 2021)

Damour, Lisa, *The Emotional Lives of Teenagers: Raising Connected, Capable and Compassionate Adolescents* (Ballantine Books, 2023)

Duffy, John, *Parenting the New Teen in the Age of Anxiety* (Mango Publishing Group, 2019)

Hohnen, Bettina, Jane Gilmour and Tara Murphy, *The Incredible Teenage Brain: Everything You Need to Know to Unlock Your Teen's Potential* (Jessica Kingsley, 2020)

Sadoc, Allan, *Parenting Your LGBTQ+ Teen: A Guide to Supporting, Empowering, and Connecting with Your Child* (Rockbridge Press, 2021)

Spargo-Mabbs, Fiona, *Talking the Tough Stuff with Teens: Making Conversations Work When It Matters Most* (Sheldon Press, 2022)

REFERENCES

Alderson, Suzanne, *Never Let Go: How to Parent Your Child Through Mental Illness* (Vermilion, 2020)

Blakemore, Sarah-Jayne, *Inventing Ourselves: The Secret Life of the Teenage Brain* (Black Swan, 2019)

Brooks, Ben, *Every Parent Should Read This Book: Eleven Lessons for Raising a 21st Century Teenager* (Quercus Books, 2021)

Candy, Lorraine, *"Mum, What's Wrong With You?": 101 Things Only Mothers of Teenage Girls Know* (4th Estate, 2021)

Cleare, Anita, *Grieving the Loss of Childhood: Hurtful Teenage Years* (Huffington Post, 21 April 2017)

Damour, Lisa, *The Emotional Lives of Teenagers: Raising Connected, Capable and Compassionate Adolescents* (Ballantine Books, 2023)

Jensen, Frances E., *The Teenage Brain: A Neuroscientist's Survival Guide to Raising Adolescents and Young Adults* (HarperCollins, 2015)

Neufeld, Gordon and Gabor Maté, *Hold On to Your Kids: Why Parents Need to Matter More Than Peers* (Vermilion, 2019)

Price, Adam, *He's Not Lazy: Empowering Your Son to Believe in Himself* (Sterling, 2017)

INDEX

ACKNOWLEDGEMENTS

I would never have written this book if it weren't for the parents who reached out to me after hearing me speak, or reading something I had written, and told me how much it meant to them. "You have shown me a path through," said one. "It was truly life changing," said another. These precious interactions (like secret handshakes) helped me find the words I wish I could have read when I was at sea in the darkest teenage years and in need of a guide rope.

I am indebted to my husband, Ivan Palmer, for his love, his unswerving support, his good humour and for taking on an unfair share of dog walking to give me time to write this book. My thanks also to my agent, Anna Power, for her persistence and belief in me, and to Professor Anthony Cleare for his expert eye.

And although I might have wished our journey through the teenage years to have been smoother, I am deeply grateful to my (now young adult) children who, in addition to being the most amazing human beings, have taught me so much about life and love and given me permission to share this with you.

ABOUT THE AUTHOR

Anita Cleare (MA, AdvDip) is a parenting speaker, writer and coach who supports working parents to balance successful careers with being a parent. She writes the award-nominated 'Thinking Parenting' blog (www.anitacleare.co.uk) and delivers expert parenting seminars, webinars and one-to-one support.

Anita has studied developmental psychology (child development) to postgraduate level and is an accredited Triple P® parenting coach. A leading UK parenting expert, she speaks at events internationally and is regularly featured as a parenting expert on TV and radio. She is Director of the Positive Parenting Project.